The Shopping Cart Test

How Small Behaviors Reveal Trust, Ethics, and Reliability in Business

Michael Wilson

Power Reads Publishing

Contents

Introduction

Y ou can learn a lot about a person in a moment most people ignore.

Picture this. You finish loading your groceries into your car. You close the trunk. You look at the empty shopping cart beside you. No one is watching. No one is going to reward you for returning it. No one is going to punish you for leaving it behind. And yet, that small decision tells a story.

Most people call it a minor act. I do not.

I call it a signal.

This book is built on one central belief: small behaviors reveal big truths. In business, most people are trained to judge others by resumes, interviews, polished presentations, and public performance. But those things often tell you less than you think. People perform when they know they are being watched. Real character shows up in the ordinary moments, when there is no reward for doing right and no consequence for doing wrong.

That is why the shopping cart matters.

Returning a shopping cart is not about the cart itself. It is about ownership. It is about responsibility. It is about what a person does when convenience collides with obligation. The person who walks the cart back chooses order over ease. The person who leaves it behind chooses personal convenience and leaves the cost for someone else. The scale of the action is small, but the meaning is not.

The same pattern shows up everywhere in business.

It shows up in the employee who notices a mistake and fixes it without being asked. It shows up in the partner who says they will follow up, then does. It shows up in the leader who owns a problem instead of hiding behind an excuse. It also shows up in the missed email, the sloppy handoff, the broken promise, the ignored detail, and the quiet habit of leaving unfinished work for other people to clean up.

Take a moment to think. How many times have you trusted someone because they sounded sharp, looked prepared, or knew exactly what to say? How many times did that confidence later fall apart under the weight of weak follow-through, poor standards, or a pattern of cutting corners? So what does this imply? It implies that many leaders are not lacking information. They are just reading the wrong information.

This book will help you read the right signals.

At its core, this book is about trust. Not surface-level trust. Not the kind built on a good first impression. I am talking about the kind of trust that allows you to hand off responsibility without looking over your shoulder. The kind of trust that protects your team, your clients, your culture, and your reputation. The kind of trust that makes a business stronger because the people inside it hold themselves to a high standard, even when nobody is checking.

No.

Trust is not built by words alone. It is built by behavior.

That is why interviews, polished credentials, and confident presentations can be misleading. They show you how someone performs when the spotlight is on. They do not always show you how that person will operate on an ordinary Tuesday afternoon when the work is repetitive, the pressure is low, and no one is watching. That is where standards are exposed. That is where patterns are formed. That is where the truth lives.

This book will show you how to spot those patterns before they become expensive. It will help you recognize the signs of reliability, the signals of entitlement, and the habits that separate people who take ownership from people who leave a trail of unfinished responsibilities behind them. It will help you stop being surprised by failures that were visible long before the damage was done.

But this book is not only about how you evaluate other people.

It is also a mirror.

As you read these pages, you will probably think about employees, coworkers, vendors, partners, and leaders you have known. Good. You should. But I also want you to turn this lens inward. Are you returning your own cart? Are you following through on the small commitments? Are you doing what is right when it is slightly inconvenient? Are you building your life and your business on ownership, or are you letting convenience shape your standards?

People are not bad, circumstances are. Still, circumstances reveal what is already there. They reveal habits. They reveal standards. They reveal whether a person is committed to doing what is right, or only what is easy.

That is why the small things are never just small things.

They are the early indicators of the person behind the promise.

My goal in this book is simple. I want to give you a practical framework for evaluating trust, ethics, and reliability in the real world. I want to help you stop guessing. I want to help you protect your business from avoidable friction, avoidable disappointment, and avoidable failure. More than that, I want to help you build a stronger culture, where ownership is normal, reliability is expected, and trust becomes one of your greatest advantages.

Come on, let's create a strong foundation together.

On the pages ahead, I will show you how to identify the signals, understand the patterns, and make better decisions about who you trust, who you build with, and what standard you expect from yourself. Once you learn to see the small things clearly, you will not dismiss them again.

And that is a good thing.

Chapter 1: The Integrity Signal: The Sniper's Lens on Behavior

The Integrity Signal: The Sniper's Lens on Behavior

Business is built entirely on the people you choose to trust. Every day, you are forced to make decisions about who to hire, who to partner with, who to promote, and who to rely on. The success or failure of your entire operation rests on the accuracy of those decisions. Yet, evaluating human character is notoriously difficult. People are complex. They project idealized versions of themselves. They say what you want to hear. If you rely on traditional methods to measure trust, you will inevitably invite the wrong people into your business.

To protect your company, you must change how you gather information. You must stop listening to the narrative people craft for you. You must start watching the quiet, mundane actions they perform when they believe no one is paying attention. You must learn to read the integrity signal.

The Sniper's Lens

During my time in the Army, I learned quickly that trust was not built on words. It was built on actions. In high-pressure situations, small lapses in discipline could have serious consequences. A poorly packed rucksack, a piece of gear left uncleaned, or a missed timeline by two minutes were not viewed as minor errors. They were indicators of a mindset. The military environment does not offer the luxury of waiting for an end-of-year performance review to determine if the person next to you is reliable. You have to know right now.

That experience trained me to pay attention to behavior patterns instead of intentions. It forced me to realize that when the stakes are low, people show you exactly who they will be when the stakes are high. It fundamentally changed how I evaluate people. I stopped listening to what people promised. I started watching what they did.

When I transitioned into the business world, I saw the exact opposite approach. Business owners constantly evaluated people based on what they said. They hired based on polished interviews. They formed partnerships based on charismatic presentations. They promoted based on loud declarations of loyalty. And then they acted shocked when these same people failed to deliver. The problem was not a lack of information. The problem was a lack of attention.

To survive and scale in business, you must adopt what I call the sniper's lens.

A sniper operates through a scope of extreme focus. They do not listen to what a target is saying. They do not care about the target's intentions. They watch the mechanics of behavior. They look for rhythm. They look for baseline habits. They look for tiny deviations from that baseline. A sniper filters out the noise and focuses exclusively on the physical reality in front of them.

If you want to build a reliable team, you must adopt this exact lens. You must strip away the noise of resumes, titles, and polished communication. These elements create the illusion of reliability. Consistent behavior is what actually proves it.

How many times have you hired someone who interviewed perfectly, only to discover they were a disaster to manage? How many times have you partnered with someone who had a flawless resume, only to find they cut corners the moment things got difficult?

These mistakes happen because we look at the wrong signals. We overvalue words and undervalue patterns.

We trust the credential. We ignore the conduct.

We trust the reference. We ignore the routine.

We trust the promise. We ignore the pattern.

This cycle must end. You must recognize that interviews are one of the weakest ways to evaluate trust. People perform in interviews. They rehearse their answers. They wear their best clothes. They are fully aware that they are being observed. High-stakes observation changes behavior. Real character shows up in unguarded moments.

This concept pushes back against a popular narrative in modern business culture. We are constantly told that you cannot judge someone based on a small mistake. We are told that everyone has a bad day. We are told to give people the benefit of the doubt.

As a leader, you cannot afford this kind of naive optimism. You can judge people accurately based on small behaviors. In fact, informed judgment based on behavioral patterns is your highest responsibility. Judgment is not about being critical. Judgment is about risk mitigation.

There is a massive difference between a snap judgment and an informed judgment. A snap judgment is driven by bias, emotion, or superficial traits. An informed judgment is driven by data. Small, everyday behaviors are data points. When you gather enough data points, a clear picture emerges.

If a potential partner is ten minutes late to a lunch meeting, you note the data point. If they dismiss the waiter with a rude gesture, you note the data point. If they promise to forward an article they mentioned but never do, you note the data point.

Individually, these look like small infractions. You might be tempted to rationalize them. You tell yourself it was just one meeting. You tell yourself they were busy. You tell yourself it does not reflect their professional capabilities.

Collectively, however, these actions are a loud, flashing signal of character. They tell you exactly how this person will treat your clients, manage your team, and handle their commitments. They reveal a pattern of low accountability and entitlement. If you choose to ignore the pattern, you only have yourself to blame when the partnership eventually falls apart. Trusting the wrong person is rarely a surprise in hindsight. The signals were always there. They were simply dismissed.

Character is visible long before results are. Most people wait for performance outcomes to judge reliability. They wait to see if the sales numbers hit the target. They wait to see if the project is delivered on time. By the time the results arrive, the damage is already done. Time has been wasted. Resources have been lost. Reputations have been damaged.

Through the sniper's lens, you do not have to wait for the final outcome. Behavior signals come first, and they are highly predictive. You can predict business behavior from everyday behavior because human beings are fundamentally consistent. How someone handles minor responsibilities is exactly how they will handle major ones.

There is no such thing as a small integrity decision. Every action is a vote for the kind of person someone is becoming. Returning a shopping cart, picking up a piece of trash in the office lobby, or double-checking an email for typos are not isolated events. They are reflections of a mindset. They represent a standard.

High-trust individuals operate from internal standards, not external pressure. They do the right thing whether or not there is recognition, reward, or consequence. They do not need an audience to maintain their integrity. They do not need a manager standing over their shoulder to ensure the job is done correctly.

Low-trust individuals, on the other hand, calibrate their effort based on who is watching. If the boss is in the room, they work hard. If the client is on the call, they sound professional. But the moment the external pressure is removed, their true standard takes over. They take the shortcut. They leave the mess for someone else. They drop the ball.

Convenience exposes character. When doing the right thing is slightly inconvenient, that is where true standards show up. It is easy to be ethical when it is profitable. It is easy to be reliable when it is comfortable. But what happens when keeping a commitment costs them an extra hour of sleep? What happens when admitting a mistake makes them look bad?

If you want to know how someone will handle a million-dollar contract, watch how they handle a minor inconvenience.

To calibrate your sniper's lens, you must actively change what you define as a test. In business, we usually define the test as the formal evaluation. We think the test is the interview phase, the quarterly review, or the big client pitch. We focus all of our attention on the main event.

You must start looking at the spaces between the main events.

The test is not the interview questions. The test is how they follow up the next day.

The test is not the quarterly review. The test is how they handle a boring Tuesday afternoon when the manager is out of the office.

The test is not the big client pitch. The test is how they treat the receptionist before the pitch begins.

This requires patience. One action is an anomaly. Two actions form a coincidence. Three actions establish a pattern. You must learn to observe quietly and document the patterns. You must train yourself to stop filling in the blanks with your own hopes and expectations. Let the behavior speak for itself.

Most hiring and partnership mistakes are preventable. They happen because we choose to be blind. We fall in love with a candidate's resume. We get excited about a partner's grand vision. We want to believe they are the solution to our problems. So we turn off the sniper's lens. We ignore the subtle red flags. We excuse the missed details. We tell ourselves that minor irresponsibility does not matter in the grand scheme of things.

But minor irresponsibility always scales. Low standards in small things inevitably lead to major failures later. A missed detail on a basic report becomes a missed compliance standard on a major audit. A failure to communicate a small delay becomes a massive operational bottleneck. A lack of ownership over a small mistake becomes a toxic culture of blame.

You cannot afford to wait for the major failure. You must catch the signal early. You must look at every interaction as a window into the core of who a person is.

Start watching. Stop listening. The truth is always found in the involuntary movements. The unscripted moments. The small decisions made when nobody is looking. When you learn to apply the sniper's lens, you stop guessing. You start seeing people exactly as they are. This is the first step in building a business rooted in absolute reliability.

Takeaway: Your greatest blind spot in business is believing what people say instead of observing what they do. To accurately evaluate trust, you must stop focusing on high-stakes performances and start tracking the patterns of behavior in low-stakes, unguarded moments.

Defining the Shopping Cart Test

Imagine you have just finished a long trip to the grocery store. You walk out to the parking lot, push your cart to your car, and unload your bags into the trunk. You shut the trunk. You are tired. You want to go home. Now, you are left with an empty shopping cart.

You have two choices.

You can walk the cart twenty yards back to the designated corral. Or you can leave it right where it is, blocking an empty parking space, or propped precariously on a curb where it might roll into someone else's car.

This simple scenario is the ultimate litmus test for human character. It is the perfect behavioral filter.

To understand why, you have to look at the mechanics of the situation. Returning the shopping cart requires a small amount of physical effort. It requires a brief sacrifice of your own time. But more importantly, returning the cart provides absolutely no reward. No one will applaud you for walking it back. You will not receive a discount on your next grocery bill. You will not gain any social status.

Conversely, there is no punishment for abandoning the cart. It is not illegal to leave it in the middle of the lot. A police officer will not write you a ticket. The store manager will not ban you from returning. There are no social or financial consequences for leaving the cart wherever it is most convenient for you.

You return the cart for one reason only. You return it because it is the right thing to do. You return it because you recognize that your small action creates order instead of chaos. You return it because you have an internal standard that governs your behavior, regardless of the consequences.

This is the essence of the Shopping Cart Test. It is a binary evaluation of what a person does when they face a task with no external reward and no external punishment. It reveals exactly what happens when convenience collides with obligation.

In business, we spend an enormous amount of time and money trying to figure out who we can trust. We run background checks. We administer personality assessments. We ask complicated behavioral questions in interviews. We try to manufacture high-stress scenarios to see how people react. Yet, the answers we are looking for are usually hiding in the everyday equivalents of the shopping cart.

Every business is filled with invisible shopping carts. These are the small, unmonitored tasks that keep a company functioning smoothly. They are the moments where an individual must choose between personal convenience and collective responsibility.

You see the test in the breakroom. Someone pours the last cup of coffee from the pot. Do they take two minutes to brew a new batch for the next person, or do they walk away and leave an empty pot on the burner?

You see the test in digital communication. An employee notices a minor spelling error on a client presentation that is scheduled for tomorrow. Do they flag it and fix it, or do they ignore it because it is not technically their project?

You see the test in shared resources. A manager takes the last ream of paper from the supply closet. Do they log the need for a reorder, or do they shut the door and let the next person figure it out?

None of these actions will make or break a career on their own. No one will get fired over an empty coffee pot. No one will receive a bonus for ordering printer paper. But these small decisions are loud, flashing indicators of an individual's operating system.

When you observe how people interact with the metaphorical shopping carts in your business, you can quickly categorize them into three distinct groups.

The first group is the Cart Returners. These individuals operate from a place of absolute ownership. They do not need to be micromanaged. They do not need to be incentivized to do the right thing. If they see a problem, they fix it. If they create a mess, they clean it up. They respect shared spaces, shared time, and shared resources. When you hire someone from this group, you are hiring a foundation of reliability. You never have to wonder what they are doing when you are not looking. Their internal standard dictates their behavior.

The second group is the Conditional Returners. These people will return the cart, but only if there is a reason to do so. They return it if someone is watching them. They return it if a supervisor is walking through the parking lot. They return it if it is a beautiful, sunny day and they are in a good mood. But the moment it starts raining, or the moment they realize nobody is looking, they abandon the cart.

Conditional Returners are dangerous in business. They are chameleons. They perform incredibly well in high-stakes environments because they know how to play the game. They shine in interviews. They say the right things in board meetings. But their ethics are entirely dependent on their environment. They require constant supervision to maintain their standards. When things get difficult, or when oversight is removed, they will always take the shortcut.

The third group is the Cart Abandoners. These individuals simply do not care. They view the world through a lens of entitlement and extreme self-interest. To them, the rules do not apply. They will rationalize leaving the cart. They will tell themselves that they are too busy. They will argue that it is the grocery store's job to pay an employee to gather the carts. They believe their convenience is more important than someone else's inconvenience.

If you bring a Cart Abandoner into your business, you are inviting a cancer into your culture. These are the employees who leave passive-aggressive notes instead of having direct conversations. These are the partners who over-promise and under-deliver. These are the leaders who take credit for team successes and pass the blame for team failures. Their entire professional life is built on leaving messes for other people to clean up.

You might think I am placing too much weight on a trivial action. You might argue that a person can be a great salesperson, a brilliant engineer, or a visionary leader, even if they occasionally leave a cart in a parking space.

This is the great fallacy of modern management. We have been conditioned to separate technical competency from character. We tell ourselves that small lapses in integrity do not matter as long as the key performance indicators are being met.

You must reject this mindset completely. You cannot compartmentalize character. Character is highly highly contagious, and it bleeds into every single thing a person does.

There is no such thing as a small integrity decision. Every choice is connected. The mindset required to abandon a shopping cart is the exact same mindset required to ignore a safety protocol on a job site. It is the exact same mindset required to hide a billing error from a client. It is the exact same mindset required to speak poorly about a colleague behind their back.

The scale of the action is different. The underlying psychology is identical.

When you accept low standards in small things, you are guaranteeing major failures later. If a potential partner cannot be trusted to do the right thing when the stakes are zero, why would you ever trust them when a million dollars is on the line? If an employee will not take two minutes to clean up a mess they made in the office kitchen, why would you trust them to handle a sensitive customer service dispute?

Convenience exposes character. True standards only reveal themselves when doing the right thing is slightly annoying. When you understand this, you realize that the most valuable data points you can gather about a person are found in the moments when they think they are off the clock.

You must start running the Shopping Cart Test in your own business. You do not need to follow candidates to a grocery store to do this. You simply need to manufacture low-stakes scenarios and observe the outcomes.

Watch how a job candidate treats the receptionist when they walk into your lobby. Do they show respect to the person with no hiring power, or do they save their charm for you?

Watch how a potential vendor reacts when you ask to reschedule a meeting by thirty minutes at the last second. Do they handle the minor inconvenience with grace, or do their frustrations leak out in a passive-aggressive email?

Watch how your current employees handle shared digital files. Do they name documents according to the agreed-upon system so everyone can find them, or do they save everything as "Document1" on their personal desktop, forcing the rest of the team to hunt for information?

These are your shopping carts. They are everywhere. You just have to open your eyes and start counting them.

The people who consistently pass these small tests are the people you want to build your business around. They operate from a place of internal discipline. They do not require a carrot or a stick to perform. They do the work simply because the work needs to be done.

When you build a team of Cart Returners, you eliminate the friction that destroys most companies. You do not have to spend your days policing behavior. You do not have to clean up unnecessary messes. You do not have to constantly wonder if your team is cutting corners when you leave the room.

You get to focus on growth. You get to focus on strategy. You get to sleep at night knowing that the people representing your company hold themselves to the exact same standard you do.

Stop waiting for high-stakes disasters to tell you who people are. Start watching the small moments. The truth is sitting right there in the parking lot.

Takeaway: Character is not determined by how people act when the stakes are high. It is determined by what they do when there is no reward for doing right and no punishment for doing wrong. Find the everyday "shopping carts" in your business, and use them to identify who operates from internal standards and who operates from entitlement.

The Fallacy of High-Stakes Performance

Most business owners operate under a dangerous assumption. They believe that high-stakes situations reveal true character. They think that putting a candidate through a stressful, multi-round interview process will show them exactly who that person is. They assume that if someone can deliver a flawless presentation to a boardroom of executives, they must be reliable.

This is a fundamental misunderstanding of human behavior.

High-stakes situations do not reveal default character. They reveal a person's ability to perform under observation. When the lights are on, people know exactly what to do. They understand what is expected of them. They understand the consequences of failure.

Because the stakes are high, they marshal all their energy to project the best possible version of themselves. They are entirely focused on giving you what you want to see.

We have built our entire corporate infrastructure around this fallacy. We design evaluation processes that act as giant spotlights. We schedule formal interviews. We conduct quarterly performance reviews. We stage massive pitch meetings. We tell people exactly when they will be evaluated, what they will be evaluated on, and who will be doing the evaluating. Then we sit back and watch the performance.

This is the theater of business. Every formal interaction is a scripted event. Resumes are curated fiction. Cover letters are heavily edited marketing documents. Interviews are rehearsed performances.

You ask a standard behavioral question. They give a rehearsed answer.

You ask for their biggest weakness. They give you a disguised strength.

You ask for professional references. They give you the names of their biggest fans.

When you make hiring or partnership decisions based on these manufactured environments, you are not evaluating trust. You are evaluating preparation. You are measuring how well someone can play a role for sixty minutes. But no one can hold a performance forever. Eventually, the formal meeting ends. The spotlight turns off. The pressure subsides. That is when the script is thrown away, and the actual person goes to work.

A few years ago, I consulted for a technology firm that was searching for a new Vice President of Sales. This was a critical role. The company needed a leader who could build trust with massive enterprise clients and manage a growing internal team. The CEO brought in a candidate named David. On paper, David was flawless. He had the right pedigree. He had the right numbers from his previous firm.

The company put David through a grueling, high-stakes evaluation process. He endured four rounds of interviews. He delivered a comprehensive ninety-minute presentation to the entire executive board. He handled aggressive objections with perfect composure. He was charismatic, sharp, and seemingly completely aligned with the company culture. The CEO was thrilled. He was ready to offer David the job on the spot.

I suggested we take one final step. I told the CEO we should drive David to the airport.

I drove the car. The CEO sat in the passenger seat. David sat in the back. During the twenty-minute drive, the dynamic shifted entirely. As far as David was concerned, the test was over. He had nailed the presentation. He was out of the boardroom. The high-stakes performance was complete. He relaxed. He settled into his default behavior.

Halfway to the airport, David took a phone call from an airline customer service agent regarding a change to his flight. For five minutes, the CEO and I listened in silence as David aggressively berated the agent. He was condescending. He used his corporate title to demand special treatment. He was visibly annoyed by a minor inconvenience and punished the person on the other end of the line for it. When he hung up, he laughed and made a disparaging remark about the intelligence of the airline staff.

The CEO was uncomfortable, but he rationalized the behavior. He fell victim to the fallacy. He told me that David was just stressed from the long day. He reminded me of the flawless boardroom presentation. He decided that the ninety-minute formal pitch was the real David, and the twenty-minute car ride was just a minor lapse. He hired him.

Six months later, David was fired. The termination cost the company a massive severance package, but the real cost was the damage he did to the team. In unobserved, daily interactions, David was exactly the person he showed us in the back of that car. He was condescending to junior staff. He demanded special treatment. He deflected blame for missed quotas. He created a toxic, fear-based culture that caused two top performers to quit.

The CEO was shocked. I was not. The signal was always there. The high-stakes performance simply blinded the CEO to the low-stakes reality.

When you evaluate people entirely on high-stakes moments, you fall into a psychological trap known as the Hawthorne Effect. In the 1920s, researchers at the Hawthorne Works factory set out to study whether changing the lighting in the facility would improve worker productivity. They turned the lights up, and productivity increased. They turned the lights down, and productivity increased again.

The researchers eventually realized that the lighting had nothing to do with the output. The workers were simply working harder because they knew the researchers were watching them. Observation changes behavior.

If you build your leadership style around formal observation, you are operating under the Hawthorne Effect. If you manage by walking around the office, your employees will look busy when you walk by. If you evaluate a partner based on how they act during a scheduled boardroom meeting, they will be prepared and polite during that meeting.

This kind of evaluation measures compliance, not integrity. Compliance requires your constant presence. Integrity does not.

You want reliability. You measure rehearsal.

You want consistency. You measure a single moment.

You want authentic character. You measure forced compliance.

High-trust individuals do not need a spotlight to do the right thing. They do not operate differently in the boardroom than they do in the back of a car. Their behavior is governed by an internal operating system. They maintain their standards regardless of the environment.

Low-trust individuals calibrate their effort based entirely on the environment. They calculate the stakes. If the stakes are high, they perform. If the stakes are low, they abandon the shopping cart.

To build a reliable business, you must invert your evaluation process. You must recognize the 99 Percent Rule.

Business is not a series of high-stakes, adrenaline-fueled moments. The grand pitches, the massive product launches, and the intense negotiations make up roughly one percent of your actual operational life. The other 99 percent is painfully mundane. It is answering emails. It is updating spreadsheets. It is fixing minor logistical errors. It is following up with frustrated clients on a Tuesday afternoon.

If you hire someone who only functions well in the one percent, you will suffer through the other 99 percent. The daily grind of business does not offer enough external validation to keep a high-stakes performer motivated. When the spotlight fades, their effort fades with it.

You must start judging people by how they act in the margins. You must look for the spaces between the formal events. That is where the mask comes off. That is where the script ends.

The test is not how they answer your interview questions. The test is how they treat the junior assistant who coordinates their schedule. Do they respond promptly and respectfully, or do they ignore the assistant because they hold no authority?

The test is not how they handle a formal contract negotiation. The test is what they do when you point out a minor billing discrepancy. Do they take immediate ownership and fix it, or do they get defensive and try to pass the blame to their accounting software?

The test is not how they act when they win the deal. The test is how they communicate a delay in the supply chain when they think you will not notice. Do they proactively alert you to the problem, or do they bury the bad news and hope you never ask?

These unobserved moments are the ultimate predictors of business success. They are the only metrics that cannot be faked. A person can rehearse an answer about their leadership philosophy. They cannot rehearse their instinctual reaction to a minor inconvenience. A person can hire a designer to build a beautiful slide deck. They cannot hide their baseline level of entitlement when speaking to a waiter at a business lunch.

When you abandon the fallacy of high-stakes performance, you reclaim your power as a leader. You stop getting fooled by charisma. You stop getting distracted by polished credentials. You stop wasting time trying to decipher what people are saying, and you start paying attention to what their habits are proving.

This requires a fundamental shift in your attention. You must become a quiet observer. You must stop telegraphing your evaluations. Stop telling people exactly when you are judging them. Let them believe the test is over. Let them think they are off the clock. Remove the pressure, turn off the spotlight, and simply watch what they do next.

The people who maintain their standards in the shadows are the only people you want standing next to you in the light.

Takeaway: High-stakes environments do not reveal character. They reveal a person's ability to perform under pressure. To accurately assess trust and reliability, you must stop measuring how people act when they know they are being evaluated, and start observing the habits they display in the mundane, unobserved margins of everyday business.

Chapter 2: The Myth of the 'Minor' Detail

The Myth of the 'Minor' Detail

You cannot separate how a person handles the small things from how they handle the big things. People often try to make this distinction. They excuse minor lapses in judgment or responsibility by claiming the situation was not important. They tell themselves that when the stakes are high, the person will step up and perform. This is a dangerous fallacy.

In business, there is no such thing as a "small" integrity decision. Every action is a vote for the kind of person someone is becoming. The way a person operates in low-stakes, unobserved moments tells you everything you need to know about their true standards. Minor irresponsibilities do not stay minor. They scale. A skipped step in a basic process today becomes a catastrophic failure in a major project tomorrow. If you want to build a resilient business, you must stop waiting for performance outcomes to judge character. Character is visible long before results are. You just have to know how to read the signals.

Convenience vs. Character

Character is not built in a vacuum. It is forged in the friction between what is easy and what is right. Most people want to do the right thing. They intend to be responsible. They view themselves as ethical and reliable. But intention is not behavior. Intention is untested theory. Behavior is proven reality.

The true test of a person's standard happens when doing the right thing becomes slightly inconvenient. This is the moment when convenience exposes character.

Think about the shopping cart in a grocery store parking lot. The customer has finished loading their groceries into their car. They are tired. The weather might be cold or rainy. The cart return corral is four parking spaces away. Leaving the cart propped up on the curb or pushed between two parked cars is highly convenient. It saves them thirty seconds. It requires zero extra effort. Returning the cart, on the other hand, requires a small sacrifice of time and energy. It is mildly inconvenient.

This is not a neutral moment. Not returning a shopping cart is a deliberate choice. It reflects a mindset. It shows a preference for personal convenience over collective order. The individual who abandons the cart decides that their thirty seconds are more valuable than the time of the store employee who has to retrieve it. They decide that leaving a hazard for another driver is an acceptable byproduct of their own comfort. They take the path of least resistance because there is no immediate penalty for doing so.

Now, translate that exact mindset into your business.

You do not want a team built on people who take the path of least resistance. You want a team built on people who operate from internal standards. High-trust individuals do not need external pressure to do the right thing. They do not need the threat of punishment or the promise of a reward. They do the work correctly because their own standard demands it. Low-trust individuals operate almost entirely on external pressure. If you are watching them, they will perform. If the client is in the room, they will dot every "i" and cross every "t". But the second they are unobserved, their standards collapse. They default to whatever is easiest.

You can predict business behavior from everyday behavior because the brain does not compartmentalize standards. The neural pathway that allows someone to abandon a shopping cart is the exact same neural pathway that allows them to hit "send" on an email without proofreading it. It is the same mindset that leaves the printer out of paper for the next person. It is the same mindset that logs off at five o'clock without documenting the CRM notes.

When you hire people, or when you partner with them, you are bringing their daily habits into your ecosystem. You are inheriting their standards.

I learned this lesson the hard way. I once worked with someone who handled big ideas exceptionally well. We will call him the Visionary. He was charismatic, intelligent, and capable of mapping out brilliant long-term strategies. On paper, he was exactly the kind of person you want on your team. But early on, I noticed a pattern. He consistently over-looked small responsibilities. He would miss emails. He would fail to attach documents. He would leave minor tasks incomplete, assuming someone else would catch them.

At first, I justified his behavior. I bought into the myth of the minor detail. I told myself he was a big-picture thinker and that small oversights were just the cost of doing business with a creative mind. I ignored the signals. That was a mistake.

Over time, those "small" issues compounded. A missed email delayed a project by a week. An incomplete task required three other team members to drop their work and fix his oversight. The minor oversights created massive friction in the business. He was the classic Cart Drifter archetype. He let his responsibilities drift into other people's lanes, expecting the rest of the team to act as his personal safety net. Eventually, the resentment on the team grew so toxic that it threatened our entire operation. The big ideas did not matter anymore because we could not trust him to execute the foundational details.

Trusting the wrong person is rarely a surprise in hindsight. Looking back, the signals were always there. He told me who he was in the first two weeks. I just chose to ignore it because it was inconvenient for me to confront the reality of his behavior.

Most people overvalue words and undervalue patterns. When a new hire or a potential partner makes a small mistake, they will usually offer a great excuse. They will apologize smoothly. They will promise it was a one-time oversight. People listen to what someone says once, instead of watching what they do repeatedly over time. But behavior does not lie. If someone consistently chooses convenience over quality in minor tasks, they will inevitably make the same choice when the stakes are high.

This is why interviews are one of the weakest ways to evaluate trust. People perform in interviews. They wear their best clothes. They rehearse their answers. They tell you exactly what you want to hear. Resumes, titles, and polished communication can easily create the illusion of reliability. But it is only an illusion. You cannot evaluate a person's true character when they know they are being evaluated. You have to watch them in unguarded moments. You have to observe how they handle the slight inconveniences of daily work.

Do they clean up after themselves in the breakroom? Do they double-check their numbers before submitting a report? Do they follow through on a minor commitment they made in passing?

When doing the right thing involves friction, pay close attention to how a person reacts. Friction strips away the polished exterior and reveals the core operating system underneath. A person with high standards will push through the friction. A person with low standards will look for a shortcut.

You must adopt the belief that low standards in small things lead to major failures later. You cannot build a high-performance culture if you tolerate low-standard behaviors. Every time you ignore a small lapse in integrity or responsibility, you are subtly lowering the baseline for your entire organization. You are telling your team that convenience is acceptable. You are signaling that the details do not really matter.

This shifts the burden of leadership. It means you can no longer brush off minor incidents. You have to view them as critical data points. You can judge people accurately based on small behaviors. In fact, you must. Informed judgment based on behavioral patterns is the core responsibility of leadership. If you refuse to judge small behaviors, you forfeit your ability to predict future performance.

When you start paying attention to these micro-actions, the world becomes very clear. You stop being surprised by people. You stop feeling betrayed by sudden failures. You realize that people constantly broadcast their level of reliability.

Look for the individuals who choose the harder right over the easier wrong. Look for the people who return the cart when it is raining. These are the individuals who operate from a deep sense of ownership. They do not view tasks as "someone else's problem." They view their environment as their responsibility. They will protect your business with the same vigilance they use to protect their own reputation.

Stop accepting credentials as proof of character. Stop allowing charisma to mask incompetence. Start looking at the friction points. When the choice is between convenience and character, watch what people actually do. Their decision in that quiet, unobserved moment is the most accurate preview of your business future. Do not ignore it. Act on it. Evaluate the pattern, set the standard, and only surround yourself with people who meet it when it is inconvenient.

The Cumulative Effect of Micro-Actions

You understand financial compound interest. You know that a small amount of money, invested consistently, grows into a massive sum over time. You would never look at a ten dollar investment and call it worthless. You know that over a decade, those ten dollar increments build wealth.

Behavior works the exact same way. Actions are not isolated events. They are the compound interest of character. Every minor choice a person makes is a deposit or a withdrawal in their integrity account.

People like to believe they can turn their character on and off. They think they can be careless in their personal life but meticulous in their professional life. They assume they can be disorganized with small tasks but highly structured when managing a multimillion dollar project. This is a delusion. The human brain does not operate in distinct, disconnected silos. The brain builds habits. It builds neural pathways based on repetition. Every time you do something, you make it easier to do that exact same thing again.

Every time a person acts, they cast a vote for the type of person they are becoming. There is no neutral action. You are either reinforcing a high standard or you are validating a low one.

When someone walks away from a shopping cart in a parking lot, they are not just leaving a cart. They are casting a vote for apathy. They are telling themselves that collective order does not matter. They are reinforcing the belief that minor responsibilities belong to someone else. It is a small vote. But if they cast that vote enough times, apathy becomes their default operating system.

When that person walks into your office the next morning, they do not leave that operating system at the door. They bring it into your meetings. They bring it into your client relationships. They bring it into your company culture.

The individual who feels entitled to leave a shopping cart for someone else to clean up will feel entitled to leave a mess in your shared digital files. They will feel entitled to leave a difficult client conversation for the account manager. They will feel entitled to log off without finishing their documentation. They have already practiced the habit of walking away. They have already voted for convenience over responsibility. You are simply seeing the professional manifestation of their personal habits.

You cannot hire a person without hiring their trajectory. The resume tells you where they have been. Their micro-actions tell you where they are going.

I once consulted for a logistics firm that needed to hire a senior operations director. We narrowed the field down to one highly qualified candidate. On paper, he was flawless. He spoke eloquently. He had the right credentials. He possessed a commanding presence that made the executive team feel confident. But during his final day of interviews, I noticed a sequence of minor behaviors.

He interrupted the junior receptionist who guided him to the conference room. He drank from a plastic water bottle and left the empty bottle on the floor next to his chair rather than throwing it in the recycling bin right outside the door. When the final interview concluded, he pushed his chair back and left it blocking the walkway.

None of these actions were firing offenses on their own. They were just micro-actions. But they were a cluster of votes. They voted for arrogance, a lack of spatial awareness, and a subtle sense of entitlement.

I recommended the firm pass on him. The CEO thought I was being entirely too critical. He argued that we were hiring a director to streamline operations, not to push in chairs. He hired the candidate.

Eight months later, the CEO had to terminate him. The new director had alienated the entire support staff. He ignored standard operating protocols because he felt they did not apply to someone at his level. He created a toxic micro-culture within his department that led to the resignation of two top performers. His massive professional failures were perfectly predicted by his minor personal habits. The signals were loud and clear on day one. The leadership team just chose to ignore the trajectory.

Many leaders hesitate to evaluate people based on small details. They worry about looking petty. They tell themselves that a messy desk, a late email, or an interrupted conversation does not define a person's worth.

This is a profound misunderstanding of human behavior. You are not judging their worth as a human being. You are evaluating their reliability as a professional. You are assessing risk.

If you ignore the micro-actions, you blind yourself to the future. You forfeit your most valuable data points. When you dismiss small behavioral red flags, you are choosing comfort over clarity. It is uncomfortable to confront a new partner about their habit of showing up three minutes late to every call. It is uncomfortable to correct a talented salesman who constantly forgets to attach the promised PDF. It is much easier to fix the small problem yourself and move on.

But what happens when you fix their typo instead of making them fix it? You validate sloppiness. What happens when you accept their excuse for a broken minor promise? You validate a culture of zero accountability. You teach them that your standards are merely suggestions.

You must recognize that a person who does not respect small boundaries will eventually violate large ones.

Think about the trajectory of a lie. No one wakes up one morning and decides to commit massive corporate fraud out of nowhere. Fraud is a destination. It is reached by taking hundreds of tiny steps in the wrong direction. It starts with a slight exaggeration on a status report. It moves to a shaved hour on a timesheet. It escalates to an improperly categorized expense. Each small lie makes the next lie easier to tell. The micro-actions compound until the individual is completely disconnected from the truth.

The same rule applies to reliability. High-performance is not an accident. It is the result of thousands of micro-actions compounding in the right direction.

Look for the team member who double-checks the calendar invite before sending it. Look for the vendor who proactively updates you on a minor delay before you have to ask. Look for the partner who picks up a piece of trash in the hallway even when no one is watching.

These individuals are casting votes for excellence. They are building an internal operating system based on precision and ownership. When the high-stakes moment inevitably arrives, they will not need to suddenly "step up" and perform. They will simply rely on the foundation they have been building every single day. Their trajectory is pointed straight up.

Your business is nothing more than the sum total of the behaviors of the people inside it. If you tolerate people who abandon the cart, your business will slowly fill up with abandoned responsibilities. Your managers will spend all their time cleaning up the messes left behind by careless employees. Your profit margins will erode as you constantly patch holes created by minor oversights.

You must shift your focus from current output to behavioral trajectory. A high performer with declining micro-habits is a massive liability. They are resting on their past success while their daily standards rot. Eventually, the foundation will collapse. Conversely, a lower-level performer with strict, upward-trending micro-habits is your greatest asset. They are building the discipline required for future mastery.

Do not allow people to dismiss their own minor failures. When someone tells you "it is just a small thing", you must recognize that statement as a massive red flag. The phrase "it is just a small thing" is the battle cry of the unreliable. It is the ultimate rationalization for poor character. To a reliable person, the small things are the job. The details are the very fabric of trust.

You cannot separate the person from the pattern. The pattern is the person.

Stop listening to the polished answers people give you in high-pressure situations. Start watching the silent votes they cast when they think you are not looking. Watch how they treat waitstaff. Watch how they handle a mildly frustrating software glitch. Watch how they organize their digital workspace. Watch how they return the cart.

These moments are not trivial. They are predictive. They are the leading indicators of business success or failure. If you learn to read these micro-actions, you will never be surprised by a betrayal, a failure, or a missed deadline again. You will see the outcome coming from miles away.

Tomorrow, pick one specific micro-action to observe in your team or your partners. Pick something completely unglamorous. Look at how they format their internal memos. Look at how they leave the conference room after a meeting. Do not comment on it. Do not correct it immediately. Just observe. Watch the pattern emerge. Once you see the pattern, you will know exactly who you are dealing with. Adjust your trust accordingly.

Small Mistakes, Big Costs

There is a dangerous phrase that echoes through the hallways of almost every struggling business. You have likely heard it. You have probably even said it yourself. The phrase is, "It was just a small mistake."

Leaders use this phrase to comfort themselves. They use it to avoid uncomfortable conversations with their employees. They use it to rationalize the creeping mediocrity in their operations. When a vendor sends an invoice with the wrong billing code, you fix it and say it was just a small mistake. When a project manager sends out a weekly update with glaring typos, you ignore it and tell yourself they are simply moving fast. When a new hire forgets to attach the crucial document to a client email, you apologize on their behalf and assume it will not happen again.

You are lying to yourself. You are treating the symptom and ignoring the disease.

In the realm of business performance, a small mistake is rarely an isolated event. It is a symptom of a much deeper operational flaw. It is a flashing indicator of how a person thinks, how they value their work, and how they respect their peers. When you dismiss a minor error as irrelevant, you are fundamentally misunderstanding how risk scales within an organization. A small mistake is never just about the mistake itself. It is about the gap in awareness that allowed the mistake to happen in the first place.

If a person has a gap in their awareness during a low-stakes task, that exact same gap will be present during a high-stakes crisis. The environment changes, but the person's operating system remains the same.

Consider the anatomy of a routine email follow-up. This is one of the most common friction points in any business. You have a productive meeting with a potential partner. At the end of the meeting, they promise to send you a brief summary of the next steps by the end of the day. It is a simple, low-stakes commitment.

The end of the day arrives. The email does not.

The email finally lands in your inbox the following morning at ten o'clock. You open it. The summary is vague. They misspelled your lead engineer's name. They forgot to link to the pricing deck they mentioned in the room.

Most business owners will completely ignore these red flags. They will focus entirely on the fact that the deal is moving forward. They will tell themselves that the potential partner is just busy, that typos happen to everyone, and that the missing link is easily fixed with a quick reply. They will excuse the late delivery because it is just a minor delay.

This is a massive failure of observation. You have just been handed a crystal clear preview of what it will be like to work with this person for the next five years.

They failed to meet a self-imposed deadline. They failed to execute basic quality control on their writing. They failed to verify the names of the key stakeholders. They failed to deliver the specific assets they promised. If they are willing to operate with this level of sloppiness during the courtship phase, when everyone is supposed to be on their best behavior, what do you think they will do when the contract is signed and the real pressure begins?

The cost of this small mistake is not the two minutes it takes to ask for the missing link. The cost is the permanent erosion of trust.

When you notice a person consistently dropping small details, your brain subconsciously registers them as unreliable. You stop trusting them to handle things independently. You begin to anticipate their failures. This creates a massive hidden expense in your business. I call it the babysitting tax.

If you hire an expensive executive, but you feel compelled to read every external email they write before they press send, you are paying the babysitting tax. You are paying their salary, and you are spending your own valuable time doing their quality control. You have effectively hired someone to create more work for you. The small mistakes they make in their drafts cost you the energy you should be spending on growing your company. A business cannot scale if the leadership is constantly patching small holes in the hull.

I saw the devastating cost of a minor detail firsthand while advising the CEO of a mid-sized manufacturing firm. He was preparing to select a new third-party logistics partner to handle his company's entire North American distribution network. This was a multi-million dollar contract. It was the kind of deal that makes or breaks a fiscal year.

We invited the final two logistics companies to present their operational plans. The first company came in with a highly charismatic sales director. He was polished, confident, and told a great story about their innovative tracking software. He handed out beautifully bound copies of their presentation to everyone at the table.

I opened the presentation. The date on the cover page was wrong. It was dated for the previous month. I turned to the second page. They had misspelled the name of our CEO's flagship product. I flipped to the financial projections. The sales director had left a placeholder note in the margin that said "insert updated freight costs here." He had printed the final copies without ever doing a final review.

The presentation itself was smooth. The sales director spoke for an hour and hit all the right emotional notes. But when the meeting ended and the vendor left the room, the CEO looked at me and immediately crossed the company off the list.

The sales director likely went back to his office and wondered why they lost the contract. He probably blamed the market conditions or the competitor's pricing. He would never believe that he lost a massive deal because of a few small typos. But he did.

The CEO's logic was flawless. He looked at the printed deck and saw a profound lack of care. Logistics is an industry built entirely on precision. It requires managing thousands of moving parts, coordinating strict delivery windows, and tracking inventory down to the single unit. If a logistics company cannot coordinate the basic details of a printed sales pitch, how can they be trusted to coordinate a fleet of shipping trucks across the country?

The small mistake was not just a typo. It was a structural collapse of credibility. The vendor asked us to trust their operational excellence, but their behavior demonstrated operational negligence. The cost of that minor detail was a multi-million dollar opportunity.

Small mistakes destroy profit margins. They do not do it all at once in a massive explosion. They do it quietly, day by day, through the slow leakage of time, energy, and client goodwill.

Think about the way your team prepares for internal meetings. This is an environment where you can observe true character because the external pressure of a client is removed. Does the project manager send the agenda in advance, or do they scramble to organize their thoughts five minutes after the meeting is supposed to start? Do participants arrive having reviewed the required materials, or do they expect to be spoon-fed the information during the call?

When someone shows up to a meeting unprepared, it is not a harmless oversight. It is a theft of time. If eight people are sitting in a room waiting for one person to find the correct file on their laptop, that one person is actively burning the company's payroll. They are signaling that their lack of preparation is more important than the collective time of the team.

When you tolerate these minor oversights, you establish a culture of low accountability. You teach your team that preparation is optional. You teach them that deadlines are merely suggestions. You teach them that someone else will always step in to clean up their mess.

High-trust individuals operate completely differently. They possess a deep internal intolerance for sloppy work. They do not view a typo as a small thing. They view it as a failure to meet their own standard. They prepare for the internal meeting with the same rigor they use for the client pitch. They double-check the email attachments before they hit send. They review the spreadsheet one last time before submitting it to the leadership team.

They do this because they understand the cumulative weight of small details. They know that trust is a fragile asset. It takes years to build and only a few careless moments to destroy.

You must begin looking at small mistakes through the lens of predictability. When a process breaks down, do not look at the immediate inconvenience. Look at the behavioral pattern that caused it.

Is your customer service representative constantly making small billing errors? Do not just issue the refund and move on. Recognize that you have a person handling your revenue who lacks attention to detail. That trait will eventually cost you a major client. Is your marketing director consistently late in delivering campaign reports? Do not just accept their apologies. Recognize that you have a leader who cannot manage their time. That trait will eventually derail a major product launch.

You cannot build a culture of excellence if you accept a baseline of mediocrity. You have to force the issue. You have to stop fixing the small mistakes for your team.

When a team member brings you an incomplete project, do not finish it for them. Hand it back. Make them correct the formatting. Make them find the missing data. Make them feel the friction of their own sloppiness. If you protect people from the consequences of their small mistakes, you guarantee they will make larger ones.

How a person responds to this correction will tell you everything you need to know about their character. A high-trust individual will be embarrassed by the oversight. They will take immediate ownership. They will fix the problem and put a system in place to ensure it never happens again. They will appreciate the standard you are holding them to.

A low-trust individual will become defensive. They will roll their eyes. They will tell you that you are being too particular. They will argue that the mistake was not a big deal. They will view your demand for excellence as a personal attack.

When someone tells you that a detail does not matter, believe them. Believe that they will never care about your business the way you do. Believe that they are a liability waiting to happen.

Starting tomorrow, change the way you audit the work around you. Stop looking only at the final revenue numbers. Look at the small steps it takes to get there. Pay attention to the formatting of the weekly reports. Watch the punctuality of your partners. Scrutinize the grammar in the client-facing proposals. Look for the gaps in awareness. Look for the missing links.

Do not brush these observations aside. Treat them as hard data. A person who ignores the small details is a person who is comfortable with failure. Do not tie your business to someone who accepts failure as a natural byproduct of their day. Demand precision in the small things, and you will rarely have to worry about the big ones.

Chapter 3: The Three Archetypes of Reliability

The Three Archetypes of Reliability

You have seen how minor actions reveal integrity. You know that a dropped detail is never just a dropped detail. Now you need a system to translate those observations into quick and accurate business decisions.

In leadership, you do not have the time to analyze every psychological nuance of the people you hire or partner with. You need a practical framework. Over the years, I have categorized the behavior patterns I observe into three distinct profiles. I call them the Three Archetypes of Reliability.

These archetypes act as a shorthand. They help you process the signals people send in their unguarded moments. When you know what to look for, you can predict how a person will operate under pressure. You will stop waiting for a crisis to reveal character and start making proactive decisions based on consistent, small behaviors.

The three archetypes are the Corraller, the Drifter, and the Abandoner. Each represents a specific level of ownership, discipline, and reliability. We will look closely at the first and most valuable of these archetypes right now.

The Corraller: High-Ownership Leadership

Picture a busy grocery store parking lot. The weather is bad. People are rushing to their cars. A stray shopping cart sits blocking a parking space.

Most people will drive past it. Some might complain about it. A few might nudge it out of the way with their bumper.

Then someone walks by, grabs the stray cart, and pushes it all the way to the return corral. They did not leave the cart there. They are not paid by the store. They gain absolutely nothing from this action. They do it simply because it needs to be done.

This person is a Corraller.

A Corraller operates from a deep, unshakable sense of ownership. They view their environment as their responsibility, regardless of their official title or job description. If something is out of place, they fix it. If a gap exists, they fill it. They do not wait for permission to do the right thing.

In business, these are your highest-trust individuals. They are the backbone of any successful team, project, or partnership.

Why do they act this way? They do not act for applause. They do not act for bonuses. They act because the alternative is unacceptable to them. High-trust individuals operate from internal standards, not external pressure. They do the right thing whether or not there is recognition, reward, or consequence.

Are you hiring people who require constant oversight? Are you managing teams that only meet the bare minimum? Are you constantly checking to see if delegated tasks are actually completed? If so, you are lacking Corrallers in your business.

I learned to value the Corraller archetype early in my career. I needed to fill a critical operational role in my organization. The stack of resumes on my desk was full of impressive credentials. I interviewed candidates who knew exactly what to say. They had polished answers. They possessed the right degrees from the right schools. They projected total confidence.

But I gave the opportunity to a reliable unknown.

This candidate did not have the strongest resume. They did not have the most prestigious background. But they displayed a consistent pattern of behavior that I could not ignore.

During the evaluation process, they showed up early. They communicated clearly before, during, and after meetings. When I gave them a minor task to test their follow-through, they executed it perfectly and without delay. They took notes unprompted. They sent a concise summary of our conversations without being asked.

These were small actions. Most managers would gloss over them and look back at the resume. I saw them as exact predictors of future performance.

Over time, this individual vastly outperformed the more qualified candidates I had hired in the past. When a problem arose, they solved it. When a process was broken, they fixed it before bringing it to my attention. Their lack of formal credentials was completely irrelevant because their standard for personal ownership was exceptionally high. They showed up early. They communicated clearly. They did exactly what they said they would do. They were a textbook Corraller.

You can spot a Corraller by watching how they handle the mundane moments in your office.

How do they act when a meeting ends? Do they leave their coffee cup on the conference table, or do they throw it away? Do they wipe the whiteboard clean for the next group?

How do they handle an email chain that is going off the rails? Do they sit back and watch the confusion unfold, or do they step in to summarize the next steps and assign action items?

How do they react to a spill in the breakroom? Do they step over it, or do they grab a paper towel?

These are not trivial questions. These are the ultimate tests of reliability. The concept of "not my job" does not exist in the mind of a Corraller. They understand that the success of the mission is their job. The health of the organization is their job. Maintaining the standard is their job.

This mindset is incredibly rare. Most people overvalue words and undervalue patterns. They listen to a candidate declare how much they care about teamwork in an interview. Then they ignore the fact that the same candidate left trash in the lobby on the way out. People listen to what someone says once, instead of watching what they do repeatedly over time.

You cannot fake being a Corraller over the long term. High-pressure situations will eventually strip away any performance. When convenience drops, true character emerges. When doing the right thing is slightly inconvenient, the Corraller still does it. They do it when they are tired. They do it when they are rushed. They do it because their integrity is not tied to their mood or their circumstances.

Compare the Corraller to the typical employee. The typical employee waits for instructions. The typical employee reports a problem and asks what to do next.

The Corraller sees the problem, solves it, and reports that it has been handled.

Which person do you want running your operations? Which person do you want dealing with your top clients? Which person do you want managing your capital?

Trust should be earned through behavior, not granted through credentials. A resume is a marketing document. A degree is a receipt of past attendance. Polished communication can create the illusion of reliability. Consistent behavior is the only real-time indicator of who a person is today.

Interviews are one of the weakest ways to evaluate trust. People perform in interviews. They wear their best clothes. They rehearse their best stories. Real character shows up in unguarded moments. If you want to find a Corraller, you have to look outside the conference room.

Watch how they treat the receptionist. Watch how they treat the waiter at a lunch meeting. Take them for a walk through your warehouse or office and see if they notice a piece of trash on the floor. If they walk past it, they are not a Corraller. If they pick it up, you have found someone worth investing in.

Small behaviors scale. The person who cannot be bothered to return a shopping cart will not be bothered to double-check a client invoice. The person who leaves their coffee cup in the sink will leave a critical email unanswered. Minor irresponsibility always scales into major breakdowns.

But the inverse is also true. The person who straightens up a messy room without being asked will catch the accounting error before it costs you money. The person who organizes the physical environment will organize the operational environment.

Do they take ownership of failures? Do they share credit for successes? Do they anticipate bottlenecks before they happen?

A Corraller owns the outcome.

A Corraller secures the perimeter.

A Corraller elevates the standard.

This is not about perfection. Corrallers make mistakes. Business is messy and errors happen. But when a Corraller makes a mistake, they do not hide it. They do not blame the system. They do not blame their coworkers. They own the failure, dissect it, and put safeguards in place to prevent it from happening again.

Let us explore the concept of internal standards further. External pressure is easy to manufacture. You can enforce rules. You can install tracking software. You can tie bonuses to specific metrics. But external pressure only works while the pressure is actively applied.

What happens when you go on vacation? What happens when a project falls into a gray area with no clear rules?

People governed by external pressure will immediately drop their standards. They will revert to the path of least resistance.

People governed by internal standards will not change their behavior. Their internal compass dictates their actions. They do not need your rules to do the right thing. They do the right thing because doing the wrong thing violates their own identity. Every action is a vote for the kind of person they are becoming. Returning a shopping cart is not about the cart. It is about ownership.

This is why character is visible long before results are. You do not need to wait six months for a quarterly review to know if someone is a Corraller. You will know in the first week. You will know by how they set up their desk. You will know by how they prepare for their first meeting.

When you find a Corraller, you must protect them. You must give them authority.

Many leaders make the catastrophic mistake of punishing Corrallers. Because these individuals are reliable, lazy managers dump all the hard work on them. The manager ignores the underperformers and overloads the high-ownership team member.

If you burn out your Corrallers, they will leave. When they leave, they will take the structural integrity of your business with them. Your operations will collapse under the weight of the Drifters and Abandoners left behind. Instead, you must recognize the immense value of your Corrallers. Reward their unseen efforts. Promote them based on their reliability, not just their tenure.

Your ultimate goal as a leader is to build a density of Corrallers in your organization. You want so many high-ownership individuals that low-ownership behavior becomes culturally unacceptable. When a new hire enters an environment populated entirely by Corrallers, they face a stark choice. They either raise their personal standards to match the group, or they become so uncomfortable that they leave. Both outcomes are a massive win for your business.

Start paying attention today. Stop evaluating people based on what they claim they can do. Start evaluating them based on what they quietly do every single day. The small things are not small. They are the honest signals of character that dictate the future of your business.

Takeaway: Audit your immediate team this week. Identify the individuals who consistently fix problems without being asked. Acknowledge their behavior immediately.

Protect them from burnout and start transitioning more authority into their hands. They are the future leaders of your company.

The Drifter: The Danger of Passive Neglect

Return to the grocery store parking lot. You have already seen the Corraller push their cart all the way back to the return bay. Now watch the next person. They finish loading their groceries into the trunk. They look at the return corral fifty feet away. They look at the empty parking space right next to their car. They push the cart into the empty space, hook the front wheels over the curb so it does not roll away, and get into the driver's seat.

This person is a Drifter.

They did not leave the cart in the middle of the driving lane. They made a minor effort to keep it from hitting another car. But they did not finish the job. They took the path of least resistance. They opted for convenience over completion.

In business, the Drifter is the person who brings a task to ninety percent completion and walks away. They mean well. They are rarely malicious. They do not actively try to cause harm. This is exactly what makes them so dangerous to your business.

Leaders often struggle to identify Drifters because Drifters are usually pleasant people. They say the right things in meetings. They agree with the overarching goals of the company. When you assign them a project, they nod, smile, and commit to the timeline.

But their follow-through is always conditional. It depends entirely on convenience. If finishing a task requires a difficult conversation, they avoid it. If closing out a project requires an extra hour of tedious formatting, they leave it messy. They do enough work to avoid immediate trouble, but they never quite cross the finish line.

You will hear common refrains from a Drifter. "I thought someone else was going to handle that part." "I got busy with another project." "It is mostly done."

These phrases sound reasonable in isolation. You want to be an understanding leader, so you accept the excuse. In reality, these phrases are the sounds of passive neglect. The Drifter lacks the discipline to follow through on small commitments. They rely on the assumption that someone else will step in and bridge the gap.

Every time a Drifter leaves a task unfinished, they create friction in your business. Friction is an invisible tax on your operations. It slows everything down. It drains momentum.

Think about the daily mechanics of your office. A Drifter makes the coffee, takes the last cup, and leaves the pot empty. A Drifter reads an important email from a client, thinks about the reply, but forgets to hit send. A Drifter updates a client file in your database but leaves out the crucial new contact number.

None of these actions will sink a company overnight. But they act like sand in the gears of a machine. Over time, that sand grinds the machine to a halt.

Who pays the price for this friction? Your Corrallers do.

The most devastating impact of a Drifter is not the work they fail to do. It is the heavy burden they place on your high-ownership team members. When a Drifter leaves a cart in an empty space, a Corraller eventually has to put it away. When a Drifter leaves an email unanswered, a Corraller has to apologize to the client and repair the relationship.

If you tolerate Drifters, you force your best people to become babysitters. This is the fastest way to burn out top talent. High-trust individuals want to solve complex problems. They want to drive the business forward. They do not want to spend their days cleaning up the careless mistakes of their peers.

You can identify a Drifter by paying attention to the final ten percent of any task. The final ten percent is where the work gets hard. It is where convenience disappears and true standards emerge.

Watch how they handle internal communication. A Drifter will forward a long email chain to a colleague with a vague note like "See below." They do not summarize the issue. They do not highlight the specific action required. They simply pass the burden of comprehension onto someone else.

Watch how they handle their physical environment. A Drifter will leave their notes scattered across a shared workspace. They will leave a printer jammed without telling the IT department. They will notice a flickering lightbulb in the hallway and say nothing.

These small behaviors reveal a deeply ingrained mindset. The Drifter believes that the final details are simply not their problem. They lack the internal standards that drive the Corraller. A Drifter operates entirely on external pressure. They will only finish the job if someone is watching, measuring, or threatening them.

As soon as you look away, their standard drops. You cannot build a resilient organization on the backs of people who require constant supervision.

I once hired a project manager who looked excellent on paper. Let us call him Mark. Mark was incredibly personable. He had an impressive resume. In his first few weeks, he seemed like a solid addition to the team.

But I began to notice a pattern of passive neglect. It started with very small things. He would lead a productive meeting but fail to send out the promised summary notes.

I would remind him, and he would apologize profusely. He would say he meant to send them and promise to do it immediately.

A week later, he submitted a budget report. The core numbers were accurate, but the formatting was a mess. There were spelling errors in the headers. I had to spend twenty minutes fixing the document before presenting it to our client. When I brought it up, he said he was rushing to meet the deadline.

These were small integrity decisions. I rationalized them at first. I told myself he was adjusting to a new role. I ignored the pattern. That was my mistake.

Three months later, the pattern scaled into a major operational failure. Mark was responsible for renewing a critical software license for our team. He received the invoice. He put it on his desk. He fully intended to pay it. But the process was slightly inconvenient. The vendor required a new payment portal login, and Mark did not have the password handy.

He drifted. He told himself he would handle it tomorrow. Tomorrow became next week. He never mentioned the bottleneck to me or anyone else on the team.

The software license expired abruptly on a Tuesday morning. Our entire operations team was locked out of their system for six hours. We lost a full day of productivity and missed a key deliverable for our largest client.

Mark did not intentionally sabotage the company. He just lacked the discipline to follow through on a small commitment. He left the cart hooked on the curb, and the wind blew it directly into the side of our business.

Trusting the wrong person is rarely a surprise in hindsight. The signals were there from the very beginning. I simply chose to ignore the unwritten meeting notes and the sloppy formatting. Most people tell you exactly who they are. You just have to pay attention.

Minor irresponsibility always scales into major breakdowns. I cannot state this forcefully enough. There is no such thing as a "small" integrity decision.

If an employee cannot be trusted to format a document correctly, they cannot be trusted to manage a high-value client account. If a partner cannot be trusted to show up on time for a routine check-in, they cannot be trusted to stand firm during a financial crisis.

How someone handles minor responsibilities is exactly how they will handle major ones.

Drifters often view small tasks as beneath them. They believe they will rise to the occasion when the stakes are high. This is a dangerous myth. You do not rise to the occasion under pressure. You default to your established patterns of behavior. If your pattern is passive neglect, you will passively neglect the big things when the pressure hits.

You must stop overvaluing words and start valuing patterns. When you interview a potential hire, they will not announce that they are a Drifter. They will tell you they are detail-oriented. They will claim they are highly motivated. You have to test those claims in real time.

Give a candidate a small, slightly inconvenient task during the hiring process. Ask them to send a specific follow-up document by a certain time. See if they do it. See if they require a reminder. See if they complete the final ten percent of the instructions.

If you already have Drifters in your organization, you have a difficult choice to make. You must set rigid, non-negotiable boundaries.

You cannot manage a Drifter by asking them to care more. Internal standards cannot be installed like a software update. You can only manage a Drifter through strict external accountability. You must inspect what you expect. You must create checklists, require daily updates, and hold them to rigid deadlines.

However, you must also ask yourself if that constant oversight is worth your time. Your energy as a leader is finite. Every hour you spend double-checking a Drifter's work is an hour you steal from growing your business. Every time you follow up on a missed detail, you are doing their job for them.

Do not let passive neglect become an acceptable standard in your company culture. If you tolerate the Drifter, you validate their behavior. You tell the rest of your team that ninety percent completion is good enough.

Once that standard takes root, it is incredibly difficult to eradicate. Your cultural standard will plummet. Your good employees will leave out of frustration. Your bad employees will stay because the environment is comfortable. The friction will multiply until your operations grind to a halt.

Protect your business by identifying the Drifters early. Pay attention to the unguarded moments. Watch what they do when they think the task does not matter. It always matters. Character is visible long before results are.

Takeaway: Identify one process in your business that constantly requires your intervention to finish. Look closely at the person responsible for that process. Stop accepting their excuses for incomplete work. Set a strict deadline for total completion. If they miss it, recognize the behavioral pattern for what it is and make a change.

The Abandoner: Signs of Active Unreliability

Picture the grocery store parking lot one last time. You have already watched the Corraller push their cart all the way back to the return bay. You have watched the Drifter hook their cart on the curb and walk away. Now observe the third person.

They finish unloading their groceries into their trunk. They do not look for the return corral. They do not look for an empty parking space. They simply shove the cart directly into the middle of the driving lane. Or worse, they leave it wedged against the bumper of the car parked next to them. They get in their vehicle and drive away. They do not look back.

This person is an Abandoner.

The Abandoner represents active unreliability. You must understand the difference between this archetype and the previous one. The Drifter fails out of laziness or passive neglect. They take the path of least resistance. The Abandoner fails out of a profound lack of respect for their environment and the people in it. They operate on a strict transaction basis. If an action does not immediately benefit them, they will not do it.

Their defining mantra is simple. It is not my problem.

In business, the Abandoner is a ticking time bomb. Drifters create friction. Abandoners create liability. They are the root cause of your most expensive legal, financial, and relational disasters. When an Abandoner encounters a problem, they do not just ignore it. They actively distance themselves from it. If a project is failing, they will not warn you. They will quietly position themselves to avoid the blame. By the time you discover the problem, it is too late to fix it.

Abandoners view responsibility as a threat. They are experts at deflection. They use company policy and job descriptions as shields to protect themselves from accountability. If you ask an Abandoner why a critical client email was ignored, they will not apologize. They will tell you that client communication falls under a different department. They are technically correct. But they are operationally destructive.

Let us look at a real scenario. Early in my career, I hired a senior sales director. Let us call him Richard. Richard came with glowing recommendations and a history of closing massive deals. He was charismatic. He knew exactly how to perform in an interview. I was eager to bring him on board.

But I ignored the early signals.

During his first week, Richard used the communal office kitchen. He microwaved his lunch, spilled sauce on the glass plate, and left it there. He dropped a paper towel on the floor and walked over it. He left his dirty coffee mug in the sink. He assumed someone else would clean up after him.

I saw this happen. I noted it. But I rationalized it. I told myself he was a high-level executive focused on big-picture revenue. I told myself that making him wipe a microwave would be a waste of his valuable time. I separated his everyday behavior from his business behavior.

That was a catastrophic mistake.

Three months later, Richard was negotiating a massive contract with a new vendor. The vendor sent over a revised agreement. It contained a critical change to the liability clause. Richard read the contract. He saw the change. But getting the legal team to review the revision would delay the deal by a week. Richard wanted his commission before the end of the quarter.

He signed the contract. He abandoned his responsibility to protect the company.

When the vendor inevitably failed to deliver, that single altered clause cost my business tens of thousands of dollars in unrecoverable fees. Richard did not care. He had his commission. When I confronted him, he did not take ownership. He blamed the legal department for being too slow. He blamed the vendor for being deceptive. He used the exact same mindset he used in the kitchen. It was a mess, but it was not his mess to clean up.

Trusting the wrong person is rarely a surprise in hindsight. The signals were there from day one. I just ignored them because I was blinded by a resume and a smooth interview.

I learned a hard truth from that experience. You can predict business behavior from everyday behavior. The person who will not clean up their own spilled coffee is the exact same person who will not double-check a binding contract. The stakes change. The character does not. Every action is a vote for the kind of person someone is becoming. Low standards in small things always lead to major failures later.

Many leaders believe they can fix Abandoners. They enroll them in leadership training. They send them to communication workshops. They write extensive performance improvement plans.

This is a complete waste of time.

You can train a skill. You cannot train character. An Abandoner does not lack knowledge. They lack internal standards. They know what the right thing is. They simply choose not to do it because it requires effort that does not serve them. High-trust individuals operate from internal standards, not external pressure. The Abandoner lacks that internal compass entirely.

Keeping an Abandoner on your payroll is the fastest way to destroy a strong company culture. Remember your Corrallers. Your high-ownership individuals watch everything you do. They see who you promote. They see who you tolerate. When you tolerate an Abandoner, you send a clear message to your best people. You tell them that integrity does not matter. You tell them that active unreliability is an acceptable standard in your organization.

Your Corrallers will not complain. They will simply update their resumes and leave. You will be left with a team of Drifters and Abandoners. Your business will collapse shortly after.

You must spot the Abandoner before you hire them or partner with them. Interviews will not help you. Abandoners are often highly skilled at managing upward. They know how to charm decision-makers. They will tell you exactly what you want to hear.

You must look at how they treat people who have no power over them. Watch how they interact with service staff. Watch how they treat junior employees. Introduce a minor inconvenience during the interview process. Ask them to wait in the lobby for ten extra minutes. Observe their reaction. Do they become visibly annoyed? Do they treat the receptionist poorly?

Entitlement is the primary symptom of an Abandoner. If they feel entitled to preferential treatment in a waiting room, they will feel entitled to ignore the rules of your business.

If you must test a potential partner or hire, use a highly structured trial period. Assign them a task with a deliberate point of friction. Give them incomplete information. See what they do.

A Corraller will ask for clarification. A Drifter will do half the work and wait for you to notice. An Abandoner will do the wrong thing entirely, or nothing at all, and then aggressively blame you for the poor instructions. When an Abandoner shifts blame, you have your final data point. Do not give them a second chance. Cut ties immediately.

You must listen to the language they use. Abandoners reveal themselves through their vocabulary. They constantly use phrases designed to create distance between themselves and the outcome.

"Nobody told me."

"That is not my job."

"I was waiting on someone else."

"They never replied to my email."

These statements are designed to stop inquiry. They are designed to shut down accountability. A Corraller says, "I have not received a reply yet, so I am calling them now." An Abandoner says, "I sent the email. It is out of my hands."

It is never out of their hands. They simply dropped the ball on purpose.

Not returning a shopping cart is not neutral behavior. Leaving trash in a shared space is not a neutral act. Hiding behind a job description is not a neutral strategy. These are active decisions. They reflect a deeply ingrained mindset of selfishness.

You cannot afford to build your business around selfish people. Business is fundamentally about solving problems for others. It requires collaboration. It requires sacrifice. It requires people who will step into a gap and take ownership of a mess they did not create. The Abandoner is incapable of this. They will take your money, they will take your time, and they will leave you with the consequences of their apathy.

You now have a complete framework.

The Corraller takes total ownership.

The Drifter relies on passive neglect.

The Abandoner engages in active unreliability.

These three archetypes are operating in your business right now. They are managing your clients. They are handling your money. They are shaping your future.

Your mandate as a leader is clear. You must elevate the Corrallers. You must rigidly manage or remove the Drifters. You must eradicate the Abandoners. Do not wait for a crisis to make these decisions. Character is visible long before results are. Every unreturned shopping cart, every dirty coffee mug, and every shifted blame is a loud, undeniable signal.

Most people tell you exactly who they are. You just have to stop ignoring them.

Takeaway: Review your roster of employees, partners, and vendors. Identify anyone who consistently uses the phrase "not my problem" or actively shifts blame when things go wrong. Recognize that their small deflections will eventually become major liabilities. Begin the process of removing them from your organization today.

Chapter 4: The Performance Trap: Why Interviews Lie

The Performance Trap: Why Interviews Lie

Interviews are the universal standard for business decisions. When you need to hire an executive, partner with a vendor, or bring on a new team member, you sit across a table and ask them questions. You expect their answers to give you a window into their character. You expect their resume to predict their future performance. You are making a massive assumption.

You are assuming the person in front of you is showing you who they really are. They are not. They are showing you who they know you want to see.

The traditional interview is not a test of character. It is a test of preparation. It measures a person's ability to perform under observation. Business, however, is not built on observed performances. It is built on unobserved execution. Real character shows up when the interview ends, the stakes are low, and no one is watching. If you rely solely on how well someone answers a question, you are walking directly into the performance trap.

The Mask of the Polished Professional

Start by defining the polished professional. They look great on paper. They have the right degree. They have the right previous job titles. They have the right formatting on their resume. They walk into the room with supreme confidence. They maintain perfect eye contact. They know exactly how to answer the question about their biggest weakness. They seamlessly spin it into a disguised strength. You leave the conversation feeling energized. You think you have found the perfect fit.

This is the mask of the polished professional.

Resumes, titles, and polished communication create the illusion of reliability. They trick your brain into equating a good presentation with good execution. You must separate the two. Presenting well is a specific skill. It involves charisma, public speaking, and reading the room. Executing well is a completely different skill. It involves discipline, consistency, and a high internal standard. These two skill sets are not the same. In many cases, they are inversely correlated.

Why would presentation skills be inversely correlated with reliability? Think about where people invest their energy. Individuals who lack the substance to do the hard, unseen work often learn to overcompensate. They realize early in their careers that they can bypass the grind if they can master the pitch. They polish their armor because there is nothing underneath.

I am not suggesting that every articulate person is unreliable. Communication is a vital business skill. The danger arises when you allow polish to override patterns. You listen to what someone says once during an interview, instead of watching what they do repeatedly over time. You let their words carry more weight than their actions.

Most people overvalue words and undervalue patterns. When you interview the polished professional, their words are flawless. They tell you about their commitment to excellence. They talk about their extreme ownership. They use the exact vocabulary you want to hear. But words are free. Anyone can memorize a script. Behavior costs effort.

Why do leaders fall for this illusion so consistently? The answer is convenience. As a business owner or manager, you are constantly solving problems. An open role on your team is a painful problem. A missing partner for a critical project is a major roadblock. You want the problem solved quickly. The polished professional offers a comfortable, immediate solution. They look the part. They sound the part. Hiring them feels like a safe decision because their credentials provide a shield against criticism. If things go wrong, you can always point to their impressive resume and say you made the logical choice.

You must stop using credentials as a security blanket. Trust should be earned through behavior, not granted through credentials.

Let us look at the resume. A resume is a heavily curated marketing document. It highlights the peaks of a career while hiding the valleys. It tells you what a person was associated with, but it rarely tells you what they actually built. A candidate can claim responsibility for a massive team success while conveniently leaving out the fact that they coasted on the efforts of others.

Credentials are the ultimate camouflage. A degree from a prestigious university tells you that someone was capable of passing exams. It does not tell you what they do when a client calls with a crisis at five in the evening on a Friday. A previous title of Vice President tells you that someone navigated a corporate ladder. It does not tell you if they leave their coffee cups in the sink for the receptionist to clean.

You cannot predict business behavior from a piece of paper.

An interview is an audition. The candidate knows the spotlight is on. They know you are judging them. External pressure forces them to elevate their behavior. They show up ten minutes early. They are polite to the administrative staff. They are highly responsive to your emails leading up to the meeting.

This is a temporary state. External pressure cannot sustain long-term behavior. High-trust individuals operate from internal standards, not external pressure. They do the right thing whether or not there is recognition, reward, or consequence. The polished professional only does the right thing when the spotlight is on.

What happens when the pressure drops? Once they are hired, the spotlight turns off. The formal observations end. The daily grind begins. This is when the mask slips. The day-to-day reality of business is mundane. It is filled with small, unglamorous tasks. It requires following up on routine emails, documenting processes, and completing minor responsibilities without fanfare.

The polished professional hates the mundane. They thrive on the stage, but they despise the grind. Because they lack a high internal standard, they begin to cut corners. When they miss a deadline, it is a small issue. When they ignore an email, it is a minor oversight. When they leave a mess, it is someone else's problem. They justify their slip-ups by claiming they are focused on big picture strategy.

Low standards in small things lead to major failures later. The person who cannot be bothered to double-check their data entry is the same person who will overlook a critical flaw in a client contract. There is no such thing as a small integrity decision. Every action is a vote for the kind of person someone is becoming.

I learned this lesson the hard way. Early in my career, I trusted a referral based entirely on reputation, not behavior. I needed to partner with a consultant for a major project. A trusted colleague recommended someone highly. This person came with a flawless reputation. Their resume was stacked with impressive names. When we met, they were incredibly polished. They commanded the room. They said all the right things about strategy, scale, and execution.

Because of their polish and the strong referral, I bypassed my own rules. I ignored the signals they were giving me outside of our formal meetings. There were early signs. They missed a small commitment to send over a preliminary document on a Tuesday, finally sending it on Thursday without explanation. Their follow-up to basic questions was slow. I noticed a distinct lack of attention to detail in their initial emails.

I rationalized these behaviors. I told myself they were just busy. I let their polished presentation and their credentials outweigh the patterns I was actually observing. I gave them the contract.

It was a disaster. The lack of detail in those early emails mirrored a complete lack of detail in their actual work. The missed deadlines scaled up. What started as a late document turned into a delayed launch. Their polished communication style turned into defensive excuses when confronted with poor results. It led to a massive breakdown in delivery and severely strained my relationships with key clients.

Trusting the wrong person is rarely a surprise in hindsight. The signals were there from the very beginning. Most people tell you who they are, you just ignore it. I ignored the reality of their small behaviors because I was blinded by the mask of their professional polish.

How do you strip away the mask? You must look at how someone handles inconvenience. Convenience exposes character. During an interview, it is convenient to be charming. It is convenient to claim you are detail-oriented. True standards only show up when doing the right thing is slightly inconvenient.

This is why the shopping cart test is so powerful. Returning a shopping cart offers no reward. Leaving it in the middle of the lot carries no penalty. It is a moment of pure, unobserved inconvenience. A person with an impressive resume who leaves their cart blocking a parking space is telling you exactly how they operate when no one is holding them accountable.

You must find the business equivalents of the shopping cart test. You need to stop looking at the polished answers and start looking at the friction points.

Notice how a candidate treats people who can do nothing for them. Pay attention to how they handle a minor scheduling conflict. Watch their reaction when you ask for a small revision on a sample project. Track their response times to routine communication. These small moments are not neutral behavior. They reflect a mindset.

If you want to hire and partner with reliable people, you must change how you evaluate them. You must accept that interviews are one of the weakest ways to evaluate trust. You cannot abandon the interview entirely, but you must stop treating it as the ultimate test of character.

Treat the interview as a baseline requirement. It simply proves the person can communicate and understands the role. Once the interview is over, the real evaluation begins. Look for the discrepancies between their words and their actions. If they claim to be highly organized but their follow-up emails are chaotic, believe the emails. If they claim to take ownership but they subtly blame their previous boss for a project failure, believe the blame.

Do not let a charismatic pitch override a history of missed small commitments. Remember that you are hiring someone to do the job, not to interview for the job.

The mask of the polished professional is designed to make you feel safe. It provides the comfort of credentials and the assurance of a good presentation. Business is not built on comfort. It is built on execution. When you prioritize polish over patterns, you invite risk into your organization. You invite people who will perform when the spotlight is on and disappear when the real work begins.

Stop falling for the performance. Stop letting a confident handshake erase a history of minor irresponsibilities. Measure the grind, not the audition.

Your next step is to audit your current hiring or partnership process. Identify exactly where you are giving too much weight to a person's words instead of their actions. Commit to finding three small, unobserved behaviors you can track before making your next major business decision. Set the trap of inconvenience, step back, and watch what they do.

Creating Unguarded Moments

You understand the danger of the polished professional. You know that an interview is a performance. The question is no longer whether the person across from you is wearing a mask. The question is how you get them to take it off.

You cannot ask them to remove it. If you ask a direct question about their character, they will give you a rehearsed answer. You must create an environment where the mask slips on its own. You must create unguarded moments.

An unguarded moment is a situation where the perceived stakes are zero. It is a moment when the candidate believes the evaluation has paused. They think the test is over. They think no one is keeping score. This is precisely when you must pay the closest attention. When external pressure vanishes, internal standards take over. If you want to know who someone really is, watch what they do when they think you have stopped watching.

You cannot sit back and hope an unguarded moment happens organically. You do not have the luxury of time. Business moves fast. You must engineer these moments intentionally. I call this structured informality.

Structured informality means designing scenarios that feel entirely casual to the candidate but remain highly diagnostic for you. You are setting up a low-stakes environment with clear behavioral triggers. You are looking for friction. You are looking for how they handle minor inconveniences, unexpected changes, and interactions with people who cannot advance their careers.

Think of the traditional interview as a spotlight. When the spotlight is on, the subject stands up straight. They smile. They use their best vocabulary. Structured informality is the act of turning the spotlight slightly away. You dim the lights. You change the venue. You introduce a variable they did not prepare for in their interview prep.

Most business leaders keep the entire hiring process contained within a boardroom or a video call. This is a mistake. The boardroom is a sterile environment. It offers no friction. It provides no opportunity to observe natural behavior. To see how someone will navigate the unpredictable reality of your business, you must put them in an unpredictable environment.

You need practical techniques to pull candidates out of their rehearsed scripts. You need to see the machinery behind the polish. There are three specific strategies you can implement immediately to create unguarded moments. They require very little effort, but they yield massive insights.

The first strategy is the administrative filter. You must pay attention to how a candidate treats people who hold no formal power over their hiring outcome. A candidate knows they must impress you. They know they must respect the hiring manager. Do they know they must respect the receptionist?

People with high internal standards treat everyone with a baseline of respect. People with low internal standards base their respect on utility. If someone can help them, they are charming. If someone cannot help them, they are dismissive. This is a crucial distinction. It reveals whether their kindness is genuine or transactional.

You must enlist your team in the evaluation process. Ask your assistant how the candidate behaved when scheduling the interview. Were they demanding? Were they flexible? Did they use basic manners in their emails? When the candidate arrived at your office, how did they interact with the front desk staff? Did they make eye contact? Did they look down at their phone the entire time they waited?

I always speak with the administrative team before making a final decision. Their perspective is invaluable. They see the candidate before the spotlight turns on. They experience the raw, unpolished version of the person you are considering. If a candidate is brilliant in your office but condescending to your receptionist, the interview is over. The condescension is their true character. The brilliance is just their act. You cannot build a high-trust culture with people who view kindness as a transactional tool.

The second strategy is the transition environment. You must change the physical setting of the evaluation. The easiest way to do this is to leave the office. Take the candidate for a walk. Take them to a coffee shop. Take them to lunch.

A boardroom is a controlled environment. A busy cafe is not. When you walk out of your office building, the candidate naturally assumes the formal interview is wrapping up. Their posture relaxes. Their guard drops. Now, you introduce the variables of the real world.

Watch how they navigate a crowded space. Do they hold the door for the person behind them? When you approach the counter, how do they treat the barista? Are they patient if the service is slow? If their order is slightly wrong, do they become disproportionately agitated, or do they handle it with grace?

I once interviewed a highly recommended executive for a critical operational role. His resume was flawless. During our formal interview, his answers were sharp, insightful, and perfectly aligned with my company goals. He was the definition of a polished professional. To finalize the process, I invited him out for a quick cup of coffee down the street.

The cafe was busy. The line was long. I watched his demeanor shift entirely. The charismatic executive from the boardroom vanished. He sighed loudly. He complained about the inefficiency of the staff. When he finally ordered, he spoke to the cashier with a sharp, dismissive tone. The barista accidentally handed him a hot coffee instead of iced.

The mistake was minor. His reaction was not. He snapped at the young worker, berating them for a simple error.

I saw everything I needed to see. I did not hire him. The boardroom showed me his ability to talk about leadership. The coffee shop showed me his inability to actually lead. If he could not handle a five-minute delay and a wrong order with basic composure, how would he handle a major supply chain failure? How would he treat a junior employee who made a mistake on a critical project?

The transition environment breaks the script. It forces the candidate to react in real-time. It reveals their baseline level of patience, empathy, and situational awareness. These are not soft skills. They are essential business survival traits. If someone falls apart in a low-stakes environment, they will absolutely fracture when the pressure of real business hits them.

The third strategy is the manufactured inconvenience. You must introduce small, deliberate friction points into the process. Convenience exposes character. You want to see how someone behaves when things do not go exactly according to plan.

You can manufacture inconvenience in simple ways. Ask to reschedule a meeting slightly, perhaps moving it back by thirty minutes at the last minute. Watch their reaction. Are they accommodating and professional, or do they become rigid and visibly annoyed? Flexibility in the face of minor disruption is a strong indicator of reliability.

Give them an ambiguous task. After an interview, ask them to send over a small piece of follow-up information. Give them an instruction that requires a slight amount of clarification. Watch what they do. Do they make assumptions and send the wrong thing? Do they ignore the request entirely because it feels like a hassle? Or do they ask a concise, clarifying question and then deliver exactly what was needed?

This is a micro-test of their working style. Business is rarely straightforward. It is full of ambiguous instructions and changing parameters. You need people who can navigate ambiguity without becoming paralyzed or frustrated. The way a candidate handles a vague email request is exactly how they will handle a vague client directive.

You can also test their attention to detail through inconvenience. When scheduling an initial call, give them two options for a time, and ask them to confirm their preference by replying with a specific subject line. This is a very small hurdle. It requires them to read the entire email and follow a simple, slightly inconvenient instruction. You will be shocked by how many highly credentialed professionals fail this basic test. They will reply with a generic subject line. They will ignore the instruction because they are moving too fast. If they cannot manage the details of an email subject line, they will not manage the details of your business.

As you implement these strategies, you must calibrate your observations. You are not looking for perfection. Everyone has bad days. Everyone makes mistakes. You are looking for discrepancies. You are looking for the gap between the person they claim to be and the person their behavior reveals.

You must establish their baseline during the formal interview. Note their energy level, their tone of voice, and their level of engagement. Then, watch for the deviation during the unguarded moments. Does their energy suddenly drop when they speak to the receptionist? Does their polite tone turn sharp when dealing with a minor inconvenience?

A high-trust individual maintains their baseline regardless of the environment. Their respect, diligence, and patience are constant. A low-trust individual experiences drastic swings in behavior. They only deploy their positive traits when they believe there is a return on investment.

You are looking for patterns. One minor sigh in a slow coffee line might just be fatigue. A sigh in the coffee line, combined with a rude email to your assistant, and a failure to follow a basic scheduling instruction, is a pattern. It is a loud, clear signal of who this person truly is. You must stop ignoring the signals.

Do not allow candidates to hide behind their polished presentations. Force the issue. Pull them out of the boardroom. Change the environment. Introduce minor friction. Ask the people around you for their observations.

Creating unguarded moments is the fastest way to separate a rehearsed performance from genuine character. It shifts your evaluation process from passive listening to active observation. It puts you back in control.

Your next step is to redesign your evaluation process. Pick one strategy from this chapter. Introduce an administrative filter, plan a transition environment, or manufacture a small inconvenience in your very next hiring cycle. Stop relying on the spotlight. Start watching what happens in the shadows.

Patterns Over Promises

You sit in the room and listen. The candidate is leaning forward. They are making perfect eye contact. They are telling you exactly what they are going to do for your company in their first ninety days. They promise aggressive growth. They promise unwavering dedication. They promise to treat your business as if it were their own. You feel a sense of relief. You think your search is finally over.

You are falling in love with a promise.

Promises are seductive. They are entirely future-focused. They cost nothing to make. They require zero immediate effort. Anyone with a basic understanding of your industry can craft a compelling promise. A promise is simply a charismatic pitch wrapped in business vocabulary.

You must stop buying the pitch. You are not hiring a promise. You are hiring a pattern.

A pattern is a historical record of behavior. It is the steady rhythm of small actions repeated over time. Promises tell you what someone hopes to be. Patterns tell you who they actually are. When you face a major business decision, you must learn to weigh a person's consistent history of small actions heavily against their charismatic pitch for the future.

Why do we value promises over patterns? The answer is hope and fatigue. Leadership is exhausting. Hiring is a massive drain on your time and resources. When you have an open position, your team is overworked. When you need a new vendor, your operations are stalling. You are actively looking for a savior. You want the person sitting across from you to be the ultimate solution.

The charismatic pitch preys on this fatigue. The polished professional knows you want a quick fix. They deliver a narrative that removes your anxiety. They speak with absolute certainty. They tell you they have solved this exact problem a dozen times before.

This certainty creates a cognitive blind spot. You want to believe them so badly that you stop looking at the evidence. You start excusing the small inconsistencies. You notice that their resume shows four different jobs in the last three years. The pattern screams instability. The promise says they were just waiting for the perfect opportunity with a visionary leader like you. You choose the promise.

You listen to the pitch. You want to believe the pitch. You hire the pitch. But you are left managing the pattern.

You must understand the law of behavioral gravity. Behavior always reverts to its baseline.

Think of the interview process as an attempt to defy gravity. The candidate jumps. For a brief moment, they are suspended in the air. They look spectacular. They are operating at their absolute peak performance. They are early. They are articulate. They are highly responsive.

Gravity always wins. The jump cannot last forever. Eventually, the candidate must land. They must return to their baseline. Their baseline is their pattern. It is the standard they maintain when no one is watching, when the adrenaline wears off, and when the daily grind sets in.

If their baseline is low, gravity will pull them down rapidly. The person who promised extreme ownership will suddenly start blaming other departments for missed deadlines. The person who promised meticulous attention to detail will start sending emails with missing attachments. You will feel shocked. You will wonder what happened to the superstar you interviewed.

Nothing happened to them. They just stopped jumping. The promise was the jump. The pattern was the gravity. You made the massive mistake of measuring the jump instead of measuring the gravity.

I experienced this dynamic early in my business when I needed to hire a senior sales director. This was a critical role. The success of our upcoming quarter depended entirely on this hire. I brought in a candidate who delivered the best interview I had ever seen.

His pitch was mesmerizing. He mapped out a complete strategy on the whiteboard. He used the perfect industry vocabulary. He promised to overhaul our pipeline and double our close rate within six months. He was confident, charismatic, and incredibly persuasive. I was ready to offer him the job on the spot.

Then I looked at the pattern. I stepped back from the whiteboard and reviewed the small behaviors I had observed leading up to the interview.

There were clear friction points. When my assistant tried to schedule his flight, he took three days to confirm his details. He claimed he was closing a massive deal and was completely offline. When I asked for three professional references, he provided two, noting that the third person was currently traveling and unavailable. During our lunch break, I noticed he subtly interrupted the waitress twice while she was explaining the menu.

The promise was elite performance. The pattern was poor follow-through, constant excuse-making, and a distinct lack of situational respect.

I was torn. My business desperately needed the revenue he was promising. It was incredibly tempting to ignore the small behaviors. I rationalized them. I told myself great salespeople are often disorganized. I told myself his aggressive nature was exactly what we needed to close difficult deals. I wanted his promise to be true.

I forced myself to trust the pattern. I declined to hire him.

Three months later, I learned he had taken a director role with a direct competitor. Within six months, he was fired. His lack of follow-through had alienated their top clients. His aggressive nature had fractured their internal team culture. The excuses he used during my interview process were the exact excuses he used to explain his missed sales quotas.

He delivered the exact same jump for my competitor. But his gravity remained the same. My competitor bought the promise. They paid dearly for the pattern.

How do you weigh these competing forces in your own business? You must actively look for discrepancies. A discrepancy is the gap between what someone says and what they do.

When the promise and the pattern align, you have found a high-trust individual. They promise to be reliable, and they show up early. They promise to be detail-oriented, and their communication is flawless. Their words simply narrate their actions.

When the promise and the pattern collide, the pattern always wins. You must treat the pattern as the absolute truth. You must treat the promise as a pleasant fiction.

You discover the pattern through observation. You look for the repetition of small actions. One missed detail is an incident. Two missed details are a coincidence. Three missed details are a pattern. You must track these small actions relentlessly during the evaluation phase.

Watch their communication rhythm. Do they respond to emails quickly on Monday, but disappear on Thursday? That is a pattern of erratic focus. Watch their accountability. When you ask about a previous failure, do they acknowledge their role, or do they immediately pivot to market conditions? That is a pattern of deflection.

You must also dig into their historical patterns. You cannot observe everything in real time. You must ask questions that reveal the past instead of projecting the future.

Stop asking candidates what they will do. Ask them what they have done. Do not ask how they handle conflict. Ask them to detail the last time they had a severe disagreement with a vendor and exactly how it was resolved. Do not ask if they are organized. Ask them to explain the exact system they used to manage their inbox in their last leadership role.

You are looking for the mechanics of their past behavior. Promises are vague. Patterns are specific. If a candidate struggles to give you specific, granular details about their past execution, they are hiding behind a pitch. People who execute at a high level know exactly how they do it. They know the details because they live in the details.

You must be willing to walk away from a great pitch. This is the hardest discipline for a leader to develop. It requires immense self-control. You will sit across from people who say everything you want to hear. They will offer you the exact solution you have been praying for. They will look the part.

If their small behaviors tell a different story, you must reject them.

You cannot build a reliable company on top of unreliable patterns. A charismatic partner who cuts corners on small contracts will eventually cut corners on your master agreement. A brilliant developer who cannot be bothered to document their daily code will eventually crash your entire system. A highly persuasive manager who dismisses your administrative staff will eventually destroy your team culture.

The small things dictate the big things. The shopping cart test proves that character is revealed in the mundane, unobserved moments. The interview is the opposite of mundane. It is a highly observed, high-stakes performance. You cannot assess character when the spotlight is blinding you.

You must turn off the spotlight. Look at the mundane details. Look at the response times. Look at the unpolished interactions. Look at the friction points.

Promises are meant to impress. Patterns are meant to expose. Let the patterns do their job. When you learn to read the rhythm of a person's behavior, you eliminate the surprise from your business relationships. You stop feeling betrayed when people fail because you realize they showed you who they were from the very beginning. You just chose to listen to their words instead of watching their actions.

Your business deserves more than a rehearsed speech. Your team deserves reliable leaders. Your clients deserve ethical execution. You secure these things by demanding behavioral proof before you grant your trust.

Stop falling for the illusion of the future. Anchor your decisions in the reality of the past and the evidence of the present. Let the polished professionals sell their empty promises to your competitors. You will focus on the quiet, undeniable truth of the pattern.

Your next step is to evaluate the people you are currently vetting. Take a blank sheet of paper. Draw a vertical line down the middle. On the left side, write down the three biggest promises they have made to you. On the right side, write down the observed behaviors that either support or contradict those promises. If the right side is blank, you have not observed them enough. If the right side contradicts the left, end the process immediately. Believe the baseline.

Chapter 5: The Referral Trap and the Bias of Reputation

The Referral Trap and the Bias of Reputation

You have built a network. You trust the people in it. When you need to hire someone, find a new partner, or assign a critical project, you ask that network for a recommendation. It is the oldest and most common business strategy in the world. But it is also a trap.

Referrals are constantly treated as the gold standard of vetting. They are not. A referral is simply an introduction. It is a shortcut to a conversation. It is an opening. It is not a conclusion. It is certainly not a substitute for behavioral observation.

When you rely solely on a referral, you offshore your judgment to someone else. You borrow their trust. You assume their standards align with your standards. You assume their memory of the candidate is accurate. You assume the candidate operates the same way in every environment. These are dangerous assumptions. You let past experience blind you to present behavior.

This chapter is about dismantling the bias of reputation. It is about learning to look past the glowing endorsement and the impressive resume. It is about forcing every new introduction to earn their place through behavior, regardless of who sent them.

When Reputation Masks Reality

Reputation is a powerful filter. It is the story people tell about you before you enter the room. In business, a strong reputation opens doors, secures capital, and closes deals. But reputation is an echo. It is a reflection of past events. It is often filtered through the subjective lens of a third party. Reality is what happens in the room with you right now. Reality is behavior. Reality is the unedited stream of decisions a person makes when they think no one is keeping score.

When reputation and reality collide, reality always wins.

The problem occurs when you let a strong reputation mask weak behavior. You see a candidate with a glowing recommendation from a former colleague. You interview a vendor who comes highly praised by a trusted friend. You meet a potential partner who carries an impressive title from a well-known firm. They bring a halo into the room. That halo blinds you to the small, everyday signals they are transmitting.

You stop watching. You stop testing. You stop evaluating.

Why do you do this? You do this because evaluating people is exhausting. It takes time. It requires constant vigilance. A referral feels like a relief. It feels like someone else has already done the hard work for you. You assume the vetting is complete. You lower your guard. You ignore the small lapses in discipline because the person comes with a stamp of approval.

This is the referral trap.

I fell into this trap early in my business career. I needed to bring on a key contractor for a major project. A trusted associate, someone whose opinion I highly valued, recommended a specific individual. The referral came with high praise. My associate told me this person was reliable, skilled, and ready to execute. I took the introduction. I was relieved to have the search over so quickly.

Because of the strong endorsement, I granted this person immediate trust. I treated them as an unproven variable who was already solved.

Then the signals started. They were small at first. The contractor missed our first scheduled introductory call by ten minutes. They apologized and blamed a calendar glitch. A few days later, I asked for a brief summary of their initial project assessment. It took them three days to respond. When the email finally arrived, it was missing a key attachment we had discussed.

These were not major failures. They were minor inconveniences. Under normal circumstances, with an unknown candidate, my guard would have been up immediately. I would have seen the missed call, the slow follow-up, and the lack of attention to detail as clear behavioral data. I would have recognized the pattern. I would have categorized them as a risk.

But this was a referral. This person had a reputation backing them.

I rationalized the behavior. I told myself they were just busy transitioning between projects. I told myself the calendar glitch was a genuine mistake. I ignored what was happening right in front of me because of the name of the person who introduced us. I valued the word of my associate over the consistent behavior of the contractor.

I ignored the reality to protect the reputation.

We moved forward with the project. You can predict what happened next. The small lapses in discipline scaled. The ten-minute delay on a phone call turned into a three-week delay on a critical deliverable. The missing email attachment turned into missing project specs that caused a breakdown in delivery. The minor inconvenience turned into a major liability. The entire relationship became strained. I had to step in, manage the mess, and repair the damage with our clients.

Trusting the wrong person in this scenario was not a surprise in hindsight. The signals were there from day one. I simply chose to ignore them. I allowed the bias of reputation to override the truth of behavior.

When you hire or partner with someone based on a referral, you are dealing with borrowed trust. Borrowed trust creates a false sense of security.

You must remember that a referral tells you how a person performed in one specific context. It tells you how they performed for one specific person. It tells you how they performed at one specific time in the past. It does not guarantee how they will perform for you today.

Different leaders tolerate different behaviors. The person who referred the candidate might have a lower standard for communication than you do. They might not mind slow email responses. They might not notice missing attachments. What they consider reliable might fall far short of your baseline for a high-functioning team member. You cannot adopt someone else's standards blindly.

You must trust your own eyes. You must observe the small behaviors.

How long does it take them to reply to a standard request? Do they show up to the meeting prepared? Do they take notes? Do they execute the small commitments they make in casual conversation? Do they communicate proactively when a deadline is shifting?

These small actions are the most honest signals of character. They tell you exactly what you need to know about how this person operates when the stakes are low. If they drop the ball on a minor task during the courtship phase, they will inevitably drop the ball on a major task when the pressure is on.

Reputation is a trailing indicator. Behavior is a leading indicator.

Do not let the trailing indicator override the leading indicator.

When you encounter a mismatch between reputation and behavior, you will feel cognitive dissonance. The candidate looks great on paper. The resume is flawless. The endorsements are glowing. But they just showed up late, unprepared, and disorganized. Your brain will want to resolve this conflict by making excuses for the behavior. You will want to defer to the resume.

You must train yourself to do the exact opposite.

You must prioritize the pattern you are observing right now. People perform in interviews. People lean on their reputations. But true character leaks out in unguarded moments. When doing the right thing is slightly inconvenient, that is where true standards show up. Returning a shopping cart requires no special skill. It requires basic ownership. Sending a follow-up email on time requires no special skill. It requires basic respect for someone else's time.

If a person lacks basic ownership and respect for time in the small things, their impressive title will not save them when the real work begins.

There is no such thing as a small integrity decision. Every action is a vote for the kind of person someone is becoming. Every missed deadline is a signal. Every incomplete task is a signal. Every excuse is a signal.

Most people tell you who they are. You just ignore it.

The problem is rarely a lack of information. The problem is a lack of attention. You allow the noise of a strong reputation to drown out the quiet signals of poor behavior.

To fix this, you must change how you process referrals. You must strip away the halo effect. When a trusted contact sends someone your way, thank them for the introduction. Then mentally erase the endorsement. Treat the candidate exactly as you would treat a complete stranger who walked in off the street.

Subject them to the same behavioral tests. Watch how they handle the small details. Look for the alignment between what they say and what they do. Do they follow instructions? Do they ask clarifying questions? Do they take ownership of their mistakes, or do they immediately cast blame elsewhere?

High-trust individuals operate from internal standards. They do not need external pressure to do the right thing. They do not rely on their past reputation to excuse their present laziness. They show up, they follow through, and they execute. They maintain the same standard whether they are handling a multi-million dollar contract or a simple calendar invitation.

Low-trust individuals lean heavily on their credentials. They expect their past success to buy them a pass on current responsibilities. They believe their reputation entitles them to lower their standards.

You cannot afford to have low-trust individuals in your business. It does not matter who recommended them. Minor irresponsibility scales into major business failures. The missed email today is the lost client tomorrow. The late meeting arrival today is the blown product launch tomorrow.

You can predict business behavior from everyday behavior. You just have to be willing to look at the everyday behavior without the filter of reputation.

Never ignore an early red flag just because the person holding it comes highly recommended. The red flag is the reality. The recommendation is just noise.

Your business cannot run on borrowed trust. It must run on earned trust. Earned trust requires a track record of consistent behavior. It requires a pattern of reliability. It requires proof, not promises.

When you evaluate your next referral, pay attention to the small things. Let the behavior do the talking. Let the actions prove the character. If the reality does not match the reputation, believe the reality.

Takeaway: Treat every referral as an unproven stranger. Thank your network for the introduction, but mentally erase the endorsement. Force the individual to earn your trust through their own consistent behavior, starting with the very first small interaction.

The Reliable Unknown

If you strip away the reputation, you are left with behavior. If you strip away the resume, you are left with the person. When you stop filtering your talent pool through the lens of pedigree, you will discover the most valuable asset in business. You will discover the reliable unknown.

Let us talk about the resume. A resume is a marketing document. It is a carefully curated highlight reel. It tells you what a person was paid to do. It tells you the names of the buildings they walked into every morning. It does not tell you what they actually did when things went wrong. It does not tell you if they take responsibility for their mistakes. It does not tell you if they return their shopping cart.

You have been taught to hire for experience. You look for the candidate who has done the exact job before. You look for the logos of prestigious companies on their application. You assume that if a massive corporation trusted them, you should trust them too.

This is another form of borrowed trust. It is just as dangerous as the referral trap.

When you hire exclusively for credentials, you fall into the performance trap. People with elite resumes know how to interview. They know how to speak the language of success. They know how to package their past into a compelling narrative. They are polished. But polish is not reliability. Polish is a presentation skill.

Reliability is an execution skill.

The reliable unknown is the candidate who lacks the flashy pedigree but possesses undeniable behavioral integrity. They did not go to the Ivy League school. They have not worked at a Fortune 500 company. Their resume might look completely average. But their daily habits are extraordinary.

How do you spot them? You stop reading their words and start watching their actions.

The reliable unknown operates with a high cart-return mindset. This is a mindset of ownership. A person with this mindset does not leave messes for other people to clean up. They do not wait for instructions to do the obvious right thing. They close loops.

In a business environment, closing a loop means finishing a task completely. It means sending the email, confirming the receipt, updating the spreadsheet, and notifying the team. It is the unglamorous, invisible work that keeps a company running smoothly.

Credentialed candidates often feel they are above this invisible work. They believe their title exempts them from the small details. They leave their digital shopping carts scattered all over your business. They assume someone else will clean up after them.

The reliable unknown never assumes someone else will do the work. They take ownership of the entire process from start to finish.

Let me share an example of how this plays out in the real world. Several years ago, I needed to hire a senior project manager. The stakes were high. This role would oversee our largest client accounts. My hiring team narrowed the pool down to two final candidates.

Candidate A was the dream on paper. They had a master's degree from a top-tier university. They had spent five years at a globally recognized consulting firm. Their resume was flawless. During the interview, they spoke with absolute confidence. They used the right frameworks. They knew all the current industry terminology.

Candidate B was the unknown. They had a degree from a regional state college. They had spent the last six years working for a mid-sized, unglamorous logistics company. Their resume was neat, but it did not sparkle. During the interview, they were polite, direct, and pragmatic. They did not use buzzwords.

If I had made the decision based on the resume, Candidate A would have been hired on the spot. But I do not hire resumes. I hire behavior. I put both candidates through a series of small, low-stakes behavioral tests during the final interview process.

I intentionally scheduled the final interviews at a secondary office location we rarely used. It required them to navigate a slightly confusing parking situation. I sent them the directions myself. The email included a specific request. I asked them to call my assistant upon arrival so we could buzz them into the secured building.

Candidate A arrived exactly on time. But they did not call my assistant. They tailgated an employee through the front door. When they sat down in the conference room, they complained about the parking lot. It was a minor complaint, framed as a joke, but it was a complaint. During the meeting, I handed them a printed case study to review. When the interview was over, they left the printed case study on the table, along with their empty water bottle.

Candidate B arrived ten minutes early. They called my assistant exactly as requested. They waited patiently to be buzzed in. When they sat down, they did not mention the parking lot. They pulled out a notebook and a pen. During the meeting, they asked clarifying questions about the case study. When the interview was over, they gathered their notes, picked up the printed case study, and threw their empty coffee cup in the trash bin by the door.

These were not major events. They were micro-behaviors. But they were deafening.

Candidate A showed a pattern of entitlement. They ignored instructions because they found a shortcut. They complained about a minor inconvenience. They expected someone else to clean up their trash. Their glowing resume was masking low behavioral standards.

Candidate B showed a pattern of ownership. They followed instructions precisely. They absorbed a minor inconvenience without a word. They left the room exactly as they found it. Their average resume was hiding high behavioral standards.

I hired Candidate B. The reliable unknown.

My team questioned the decision at first. They felt we were taking a risk by passing on the pedigree. They were wrong. Candidate B became the most effective project manager in our company's history. They never dropped a ball. They never missed a deadline. They anticipated problems before they happened. They closed every loop.

We tracked Candidate A out of curiosity. Over the next three years, they bounced between three different agencies. Their reputation got them through the door, but their behavior could not keep them in the room.

Why do leaders so often choose the credential over the character? The answer is fear.

Leaders hire the pedigree because it feels safe. It is a defensive strategy. If you hire the Ivy League candidate and they fail, you can blame the candidate. You can say you made the logical choice. The board will not question you. The investors will not question you. You bought the best resume on the market.

If you hire the reliable unknown and they fail, you have to take the blame. You took a risk. You bypassed the obvious choice. The failure is entirely on your shoulders.

Defensive hiring creates mediocre companies. You cannot build a high-trust, high-performance team by protecting your own ego. You must be willing to look past the shiny exterior and evaluate the raw material underneath.

When you start prioritizing behavior over credentials, you will notice a shift in your organization. You will stop managing egos and start managing outcomes.

The reliable unknown brings three distinct advantages to your business.

First, they have high agency. High agency is the ability to figure things out without waiting for a manual. Credentialed candidates often rely on established systems. They are used to working in massive corporations where every process is documented. Put them in an ambiguous situation, and they freeze. The reliable unknown is used to making things work with limited resources. They do not wait to be told what to do. They see a problem, and they solve it.

Second, they have low entitlement. They know they do not have the fancy logos on their resume. They know they have to prove themselves through their work. They do not expect a promotion just because they showed up for six months. They are willing to do the unglamorous tasks because they understand that every task matters. They return the shopping cart because it is the right thing to do, not because someone is watching.

Third, they are obsessive about closing loops. This is the hallmark of the cart-return mindset. They double-check their work. They confirm receipt. They follow up. You never have to wonder if a task was completed. You never have to send an email asking for an update. The reliable unknown communicates proactively.

These three traits are worth a hundred times more than a prestigious degree. But you will never find these traits if you only look at resumes. You have to design your vetting process to expose them.

You must create low-stakes behavioral tests.

Do not ask a candidate to tell you about a time they showed attention to detail. That is a meaningless question. They will give you a rehearsed answer. Instead, test their attention to detail in real time. Give them a task with a minor error in it. See if they catch it. Send them an email with three distinct questions. See if they answer all three, or if they only answer the first one and ignore the rest.

Watch how they treat the people who have no power over them. Do they greet the receptionist? Do they thank the person who brings them water? Do they clean up after themselves?

Pay attention to their response times. Do they reply to scheduling emails promptly? Do they send a follow-up after the meeting? Do they deliver requested materials exactly when they promised?

These are the signals that matter. A candidate who respects time, follows instructions, and takes ownership of small details will bring those exact same habits to your biggest projects.

A candidate who misses deadlines, ignores instructions, and expects others to clean up their messes will bring those exact same habits to your biggest projects.

The reliable unknown is out there. They are sitting in your applicant pool right now. They are the vendor you scrolled past because their website was not as flashy as their competitors. They are the potential partner who does not have a massive social media following.

They are quietly doing the work. They are operating with internal standards. They are doing the right thing when no one is watching.

Your job is to find them. Your job is to ignore the noise of the reputation and focus entirely on the signal of the behavior.

Stop overvaluing words. Stop overvaluing past associations. Start valuing patterns.

When you find a person who consistently executes in the small things, pull them close. Give them responsibility. Give them opportunity. They will outperform the credentialed candidate every single time.

Character is visible long before results are. You just have to know what you are looking for. You have to be willing to trust your own eyes. You have to be willing to bet on the behavior.

Takeaway: Stop hiring defensive resumes and start hiring for high agency and low entitlement. Design your vetting process to include low-stakes behavioral tests that reveal a candidate's true habits before you ever extend an offer.

Trust is Earned, Not Granted

"I trust people until they give me a reason not to."

You have likely heard this phrase. You have likely said it yourself. It sounds magnanimous. It sounds like the philosophy of an optimistic and empowering leader. It feels good to say. But in business, it is a massive vulnerability. It is a lazy approach to leadership. It assumes everyone operates with your internal standards until proven otherwise.

When you trust someone by default, you are granting trust. You are handing over the keys to your resources, your clients, and your reputation before the person has proven they know how to drive. You are making a blind investment based on hope.

Trust should never be granted. Trust must be earned.

This requires a fundamental shift in your leadership mindset. You must stop viewing trust as a default setting and start viewing it as a destination. You must force every new hire, every new partner, and every new vendor to walk the path to get there. You must require behavioral evidence before you give them access to the things that matter most in your business.

Why do leaders grant trust so easily? They do it out of convenience. Evaluating people is exhausting. Managing people is exhausting. When you finally sign a contract with a new vendor or hire a new manager, you want to believe the hard work is over. You want to delegate the problem and get back to your own work. You want to assume the person will do exactly what they promised in the interview.

Your optimism becomes your blind spot. You confuse a good conversation with a track record of execution.

Granted trust creates a structural flaw in your business. When you give full autonomy to an unproven individual, you are setting a trap for yourself. If they fail, the damage is immediate and severe. They do not fail in a small, contained way. They fail on your biggest accounts. They drop the ball on your most critical deadlines. Because you granted them full access upfront, their minor irresponsibility instantly becomes a major business liability.

You also create a psychological trap for yourself. Once you grant trust, taking it away feels like a punishment. If a new manager makes a mistake and you suddenly start micromanaging them, they will resent you. They will feel like you are moving the goalposts. You will feel like a tyrant.

If you never grant the trust in the first place, you never have to take it away. You simply delay the reward of autonomy until the behavior justifies it.

You must separate respect from trust. This is a critical distinction. You owe every new person in your orbit absolute respect from day one. You respect their time. You respect their dignity. You respect their ideas. You treat them as a valued professional. But you do not owe them your trust. Respect is the baseline of human interaction. Trust is the currency of business execution.

To shift to an earned-trust mindset, you must start everyone at zero.

Starting at zero does not mean you are cynical. It does not mean you are waiting for people to fail. It simply means you are operating as an objective observer. You are acknowledging that you do not yet know the pattern of this person. You are refusing to substitute a strong resume or a glowing referral for actual, observed behavior.

You build earned trust through behavioral gating.

Behavioral gating is the practice of locking your most valuable assets behind doors that only consistent behavior can open. You do not hand over the entire project. You hand over a piece of the project. You set a clear expectation. You define the standard of execution. Then, you step back and watch what happens.

I applied this exact framework a few years ago when I needed to hire a specialized marketing agency for a massive product launch. The agency had incredible credentials. They worked with massive brands. Their pitch deck was flawless. The referral came from a highly successful peer. Everything on paper told me to sign their annual retainer and let them take control.

My default setting wanted to grant them trust. I was busy. I wanted the marketing problem solved. But I forced myself to pause. I forced myself to start at zero.

Instead of signing the massive annual contract, I proposed a paid, two-week test pilot. I carved out a tiny fraction of the budget. I gave them a very specific, low-stakes objective. I also gave them one simple administrative instruction. I told the account manager I needed a daily text message by five o'clock every afternoon with the exact ad spend and the exact lead count for the day. Nothing complex. No fancy charts. Just two numbers in a text message.

This was my behavioral gate. It was a simple shopping cart test for a corporate partner.

On day one, the text message arrived at 5:45 PM. On day two, there was no text message at all. I received an email the next morning at nine o'clock with a long, rambling excuse about an API integration issue on their dashboard. On day three, the text message arrived, but it only contained the lead count, not the ad spend.

Their strategy might have been brilliant. Their creative design might have been award-winning. But their behavior was fundamentally broken. They could not follow a simple, low-stakes instruction. They could not close a basic communication loop. They lacked the micro-disciplines required for high-level execution.

I did not sign the annual retainer. I paid them for the two weeks and walked away.

The agency was shocked. They argued that the daily text message was an insignificant detail. They argued that I was missing the big picture. They did not understand my framework. I was not evaluating their ability to send a text message. I was evaluating their pattern of reliability. If they could not manage a daily text message during the courtship phase, they would inevitably mismanage a multi-million dollar budget during the execution phase.

By forcing them to earn my trust in a low-stakes environment, I protected my business from a high-stakes disaster. I kept the gates closed because their behavior did not warrant the keys.

You must implement behavioral gating in your own organization.

When you hire a new employee, do not immediately assign them your most demanding client. Assign them an internal research project. Give them a strict deadline. Watch how they manage their time. Watch how they ask questions. Do they wait until the last minute to tell you they are stuck? Do they bring you problems, or do they bring you proposed solutions?

When you bring on a new vendor, give them a small, non-critical task before you integrate them into your core systems. Check their attention to detail. Verify their billing accuracy. Measure their response time to mundane inquiries.

You are looking for the shopping cart mindset. You are looking for the unprompted execution of small responsibilities.

High-trust individuals love behavioral gating. They welcome the opportunity to prove themselves. They do not want to be judged on their resume. They want to be judged on their output. When you set clear, low-stakes expectations, the high-trust individual will exceed them. They will send the text message at 4:55 PM. They will close every loop. They will show you their internal standards.

Low-trust individuals hate behavioral gating. They feel insulted by it. They believe their past reputation should exempt them from present testing. They will complain about the small details. They will make excuses for their lapses. They will try to redirect your attention back to their impressive credentials.

When a person gets defensive about a small behavioral test, they are giving you a massive signal. They are telling you that their ego is larger than their work ethic. Listen to that signal.

Shifting to an earned-trust mindset also transforms your team culture.

Your top performers are watching how you manage people. They know who the weak links are. They see the dropped balls. They see the missed deadlines. If they see you granting trust and autonomy to new people who have not earned it, your top performers will lose respect for you. They will feel that their own hard work is undervalued. They will realize that your standards are merely suggestions.

But when your team sees you requiring behavioral proof, their respect for you will skyrocket. They will know that your trust actually means something. They will know that autonomy is a privilege reserved for those who execute consistently. You elevate the entire organization by making trust an exclusive asset.

Earning trust takes time. It cannot be rushed. It requires patience from the leader. You must be willing to sit in the discomfort of observation. You must be willing to verify the small details, even when you want to look away.

You must watch for consistency. Anyone can fake high standards for a day. Anyone can return the shopping cart when the boss is watching. You are looking for what happens on day fourteen. You are looking for what happens when the initial enthusiasm wears off and the daily grind sets in.

Does the communication remain sharp? Do the deadlines hold? Does the ownership persist?

When the pattern holds over time, the gate opens. You grant the autonomy. You hand over the critical project. You introduce them to the key client. You do this with absolute confidence because you are no longer relying on hope. You are relying on data. You are relying on a verified pattern of behavior.

This is how you build an unbreakable business. You build it slowly. You build it on a foundation of verified integrity. You refuse to let impressive words override inconsistent actions. You refuse to let a strong reputation mask weak habits.

You hold the line. You keep the gates locked. You demand the proof.

Takeaway: Never grant trust based on a resume, an interview, or a referral. Force every new hire and partner to earn their access through behavioral gating. Start them at zero, give them low-stakes tests, and only increase their autonomy when their consistent actions prove their reliability.

Chapter 6: Leadership by Example: Setting the Standard

Leadership by Example: Setting the Standard

You have learned how to evaluate the individuals in your orbit. You have scrutinized candidates, assessed partners, and filtered for the internal standards that define high-trust behavior. You now hold the framework to spot patterns before they become liabilities. You can identify the Cart Finishers and the Cart Abandoners within your ranks.

Evaluation is only the first half of your responsibility. The second half is the environment you build.

You cannot demand high standards if you do not personally model them. Culture is not the list of core values printed on your office wall. Culture is the sum of the behaviors you tolerate and the actions you demonstrate. Your team is constantly watching you. They do not listen to your words during all-hands meetings: they watch your actions in the quiet moments. They observe how you handle the minor inconveniences of your daily schedule.

If you want an organization filled with people who return their shopping carts, you must be the ultimate example of that behavior. You must set the baseline. You must show your team that no task is too small, no detail is too minor, and no standard is negotiable.

The Chief Corraller

Every high-performing organization has a Chief Corraller. This is not a formal job title: it is a behavioral baseline. The Chief Corraller is the leader who takes absolute ownership of the environment, regardless of their rank or formal responsibilities.

As a business owner or executive, you hold the ultimate authority. You have the power to delegate almost anything. You can assign the administrative work, you can hand off the client disputes, and you can hire staff to maintain the office. Delegation is necessary for growth. You cannot scale a company if you are stuck performing lower-level tasks.

There is a sharp difference between delegating a workflow and abdicating your standard.

When you abdicate your standard, you adopt a mindset that small details are beneath you. You walk past a piece of trash in the hallway because you employ a cleaning crew. You ignore a typo in a public-facing document because you have a marketing team. You leave your coffee mug on the conference room table because an assistant will eventually pick it up.

These actions seem insignificant, but they are not. They are massive signals to your entire organization.

Remember the core premise of the shopping cart test: convenience exposes character. When you bypass a small responsibility simply because it is inconvenient or because it is not technically your job, you give everyone else permission to do the same. You introduce a mindset of indifference into your company culture. This mindset eventually turns into the phrase, "That is not my job."

Once that phrase takes root, your business will begin to decay. The Cart Drifters in your organization will feel justified in their sloppy work. The Cart Abandoners will take advantage of the lowered expectations. The Cart Finishers will grow frustrated, they will lose trust in your leadership, and they will eventually leave for an organization that shares their high internal standards.

To prevent this, you must adopt the identity of the Chief Corraller. You must be the one who straightens the chairs after a meeting. You must be the one who picks up the stray piece of paper on the floor. You must be the one who flags the minor error in the spreadsheet. You do these things not because you have the time, but because you cannot afford the cultural cost of ignoring them.

I observed a leader early in my career who perfectly embodied this concept. This individual took absolute responsibility for everything in their environment. It did not matter if the issue was directly assigned to them or not. If they saw a problem, they fixed it. If they noticed a gap in communication, they closed it. They consistently followed through, they elevated the baseline, and they raised standards without ever being asked.

One afternoon, a minor logistical failure occurred in our department. It was a small oversight regarding equipment storage. It was an issue that most executives would have ignored or blamed on a junior staff member. This leader did neither. They quietly stepped in, they reorganized the staging area, and they ensured the equipment was properly secured. They did not write a memo. They did not call a team meeting to scold anyone. They simply fixed the problem to the standard they expected.

Their team trusted them completely because their actions were consistent. The team knew this leader would never ask them to maintain a standard that the leader was unwilling to maintain themselves.

That is the power of the Chief Corraller. You lead through unobserved action. When your team sees you doing the small things right, they subconsciously align their own behavior to match yours. You remove their excuses. You eliminate their ability to rationalize laziness. If the owner of the company has the time to put the shopping cart away, the junior associate certainly does, too.

Your everyday behavior is the ceiling for your team's behavior. If you operate at ninety percent integrity on the small details, your management team will operate at eighty percent. Your frontline workers will operate at seventy percent. Drift happens naturally as it moves down the chain of command. The only way to ensure high standards at the bottom is to model flawless standards at the top.

Think about the physical environment of your business. If you own a retail store, are the shelves perfectly aligned? If you run a warehouse, are the aisles clear of debris? If you manage a digital agency, are the shared company drives organized and properly labeled?

These are not administrative issues: these are leadership issues.

When you walk through your business and ignore a mess, you have just endorsed that mess. You have established a new, lower standard. Your silence is approval. Your inaction is permission.

Most people overvalue words and undervalue patterns. You might stand in front of your employees and give a passionate speech about excellence, attention to detail, and customer service. They will clap. They will nod. Then they will watch what you do when you step off the stage. They will watch how you treat the receptionist. They will watch how quickly you reply to internal emails. They will watch whether you leave the breakroom cleaner than you found it.

Your words are a claim. Your actions are the proof.

High-trust individuals operate from internal standards, not external pressure. As a leader, you do not have external pressure. No one is managing you. No one is going to write you up for leaving your metaphorical cart in the middle of the parking lot. This means your behavior is the purest reflection of your true character.

If you only do the right thing when clients or investors are watching, you are a performance-based leader. Your team will figure this out quickly. They will learn to perform when you are watching and slack off when you are not. You will create an environment of compliance rather than an environment of commitment.

To build a culture of commitment, you must do the right thing when there is zero recognition, zero reward, and zero consequence for doing the wrong thing.

You build trust by consistently choosing the slightly harder path. You build trust by doing the things that do not scale. You build trust by proving to your team that you are a Cart Finisher at your core.

How do you implement this today? It starts with observation. You must begin looking for the shopping carts in your own business.

Look for the small tasks that everyone else is ignoring. Look for the unresolved client emails sitting in the shared inbox. Look for the messy formatting in the weekly report. Look for the physical clutter in your workspace.

When you find these things, do not immediately delegate them. Fix one of them yourself. Take the extra thirty seconds to resolve the issue completely. Do it quietly. Do not ask for credit. Let your team notice the standard you are setting.

Next, audit your own recent behavior. Have you been slipping on the minor details? Have you been late to internal meetings because you view your time as more valuable than your team's time? Have you been slow to provide feedback? Have you been leaving small problems for others to solve?

If you have, correct your behavior immediately. You cannot hold others accountable if your own baseline is flawed.

Finally, reframe your perspective on leadership. Leadership is not about being too important to do the small jobs. Leadership is about realizing that the small jobs are what hold the big jobs together.

The people you want in your organization, the reliable, ethical, high-trust individuals, want to work for a Chief Corraller. They want to work for someone who cares as much as they do. When they see you maintaining the standard in the minor details, their respect for you will deepen. They will trust your judgment in the major decisions because you have proven your reliability in the everyday moments.

Every action is a vote for the kind of person you are becoming. Every action is also a vote for the kind of company you are building. Decide today that you will not walk past a mistake. Decide that you will not leave a mess for someone else to clean. Decide that you will do the right thing, especially when it is slightly inconvenient.

You are the leader. You set the standard. Return the cart.

Moving From Pressure to Internal Standards

You have established yourself as the Chief Corraller. You have taken ownership of your environment. You are modeling the behavior you want to see. This is the mandatory first step, but it is not the final destination.

If you are the only person in your organization picking up the stray details, you have a major problem. You have become a babysitter rather than a business leader. A business that relies solely on the owner to enforce basic standards is a fragile business. It cannot scale. It cannot operate effectively when you are out of the office. It will collapse under its own weight the moment you turn your attention away.

Your ultimate goal is to build a team that no longer requires your constant surveillance. You need an organization filled with people who return the shopping cart entirely on their own. You need a team that does the right thing because of who they are, not because they are being monitored.

To achieve this, you must understand the stark difference between external pressure and internal standards.

External pressure is compliance. It is the employee who arrives on time only because the time clock tracks their exact entry. It is the salesperson who hits their quota only to secure their commission check. It is the team member who cleans up their workspace only because a supervisor is scheduled to walk through the building.

When behavior is driven by external pressure, the standard is entirely dependent on the threat of consequence or the promise of a reward. Remove the threat, and the standard drops. Remove the reward, and the effort stops.

Internal standards are about identity.

An individual with high internal standards does the right thing because doing the wrong thing feels unacceptable to them. They format a document perfectly, even if the client will not notice the difference, because their name is on it. They follow up on a customer complaint, even when the shift is over, because they refuse to leave a problem unresolved. They return the shopping cart to the corral in an empty parking lot in the pouring rain. They do this because leaving it in an empty space violates their own code of conduct.

You cannot build a high-trust organization with people who rely on external pressure. The tax of managing them is simply too high.

When you hire people who lack internal standards, you are forced to build expensive, time-consuming systems to monitor them. You have to implement complex tracking software. You have to schedule endless check-in meetings. You have to hire layers of middle management simply to verify that basic tasks are being completed. You spend your days managing behavior instead of driving growth.

You must stop relying on external pressure to force performance. You must pivot your entire strategy toward hiring and cultivating people who operate from internal standards.

This transition begins with your hiring process. As we established in earlier chapters, interviews are notoriously weak at evaluating true character. Candidates perform in interviews. They tell you exactly what you want to hear. Every single candidate will claim to have high standards. They will claim to be detail-oriented. They will claim to take ownership.

You must ignore their claims. You must test their baseline.

You cannot train a core value into a person. You cannot take a Cart Abandoner and send them to a weekend seminar to transform them into a Cart Finisher. The internal drive to do the right thing is cultivated over a lifetime. It is established long before the candidate sits across from your desk. Your job is not to build internal standards in your employees. Your job is to filter for them.

To do this, you must build unobserved moments into your hiring and trial processes. You need to see how a candidate acts when they believe no one is keeping score.

I once consulted for a logistics company that was struggling to hire reliable operations managers. They kept hiring candidates with flawless resumes and polished interview skills. Within three months, these new hires were routinely making careless errors and letting standards slip. The company was relying on external pressure to keep the managers in line. It was not working.

I advised the CEO to change the evaluation process. We stopped focusing on the interview and created a paid trial project instead.

We brought the top candidates in for a single day of consulting. We gave each candidate a set of real operational data to analyze. We intentionally built a minor structural flaw into the data set. It was a clear formatting error that made the analysis slightly more difficult to execute. It was not the core focus of the project, but it was an obvious mess.

We then stepped out of the room and left the candidates entirely alone to complete the work.

The candidates driven by external pressure simply ignored the mess. They worked around the formatting error. They completed the exact task they were assigned, and they did nothing more. They assumed that fixing the data was not their job.

The candidate driven by internal standards had a completely different approach. Before they began the assigned analysis, they spent ten minutes fixing the underlying formatting error. They cleaned up the data. They organized the spreadsheet. They could not tolerate working inside a messy system. They did not ask for permission. They did not point it out later to earn praise. They just fixed it because their internal baseline demanded it.

That is the candidate you hire. You filter for the people who fix the small, unassigned problems when no one is watching.

Once you learn how to identify these individuals, your role as a leader fundamentally changes. You must transition from enforcing rules to cultivating an environment where high standards can thrive. The fastest way to destroy a high-trust employee is to manage them with low-trust systems.

If you hire someone with high internal standards and then subject them to obsessive surveillance, you will insult them. High-trust individuals resent external pressure. They do not need you to track their keystrokes. They do not need you to remind them to double-check their work. They are already harder on themselves than you could ever be.

When you treat a high-trust employee like a liability, they will eventually leave. They will seek out an organization that recognizes their character and grants them the autonomy they deserve.

To cultivate these individuals, you must manage them by outcomes and standards, not by process and surveillance. Give them a clear objective. Define the baseline standard of quality. Then, get out of their way. Let their internal drive handle the execution.

You must also recognize and celebrate unprompted ownership.

Most companies praise the wrong behaviors. They celebrate the employee who works until midnight to fix a massive crisis. They throw a party for the team that pulls off a miraculous, last-minute save. This creates a dangerous incentive structure. It teaches your team that they will only be recognized for dramatic, high-stress interventions.

High-trust individuals rarely create dramatic interventions. They prevent the crisis from happening in the first place. They notice the small discrepancy in the contract three weeks before the deadline. They quietly correct the inventory error before it impacts the client. They return the cart before it rolls into another car.

Because this behavior is quiet, it is often ignored. You must change this dynamic. You must train yourself to notice the invisible work. When you see an employee fix a small problem that was not their responsibility, acknowledge it. You do not need to throw a parade. A simple, direct acknowledgment is enough. Tell them that you noticed their attention to detail. Tell them that their proactive behavior is the exact standard you expect in your company.

When you celebrate the quiet maintenance of high standards, you reinforce the culture. You prove to your team that doing the right thing is valued, even when the stakes are low.

However, cultivating this environment also requires making difficult decisions about the people who refuse to meet the standard.

When you shift from external pressure to internal standards, the Cart Drifters and Cart Abandoners in your organization will be exposed. Without your constant micromanagement, their performance will drop. They will miss deadlines. They will deliver sloppy work. They will walk past the metaphorical trash on the floor.

You cannot ignore this. Tolerance is an endorsement.

If you allow a low-trust employee to operate without consequence, you will poison the high-trust employees around them. High performers despise working with low performers. It violates their internal code. If they see you tolerating laziness, their respect for you will evaporate. They will realize that your high standards are just words.

When an employee repeatedly proves that they lack internal standards, you must remove them. You cannot afford to keep people who only do their jobs when you are holding a magnifying glass over their desks.

You must treat repeated, minor irresponsibility as a major breach of trust. Remember that there is no such thing as a small integrity decision. An employee who consistently takes the easy way out on minor tasks is telling you exactly who they are. They are showing you their true baseline. Do not wait for them to make a catastrophic error before you take action. Address the pattern early.

Shifting a team from external pressure to internal standards is not a fast process. It requires relentless consistency from you.

It starts with your behavior as the Chief Corraller. It continues with how you filter candidates during the hiring process. It solidifies in how you manage, recognize, and protect the high-trust individuals on your team.

Take a hard look at your current organization. Ask yourself how much time you spend enforcing basic compliance. How many systems exist purely to catch people doing the wrong thing? How many employees would immediately drop their standards if you went on vacation for a month?

The answers to these questions will reveal the true health of your company culture.

If your business relies entirely on your presence to maintain quality, you have built a culture of pressure. It is time to dismantle it. Stop treating your team like children who need to be watched. Stop rewarding the minimum required effort. Stop ignoring the quiet, unprompted ownership of your best people.

Demand more. Create an environment where high standards are the only acceptable baseline. Hire the people who return their carts. Fire the ones who do not.

When you fill your organization with individuals governed by internal standards, everything changes. The friction disappears. The micromanagement ends. The trust deepens. You will finally have a team you can rely on completely, even when you are not in the room.

The Accountability Loop

You have taken on the role of the Chief Corraller. You have begun filtering your hires for internal standards rather than relying on external pressure. These are massive steps forward. But the true test of an organization is not what happens when you set a standard. The true test is what happens when someone breaks it.

Culture is not a static achievement: it is a living ecosystem. It requires constant maintenance. If you step away from a garden, weeds will grow. If you stop enforcing a standard, apathy will spread. You cannot rely on your presence alone to keep the weeds out. You need a system that sustains itself.

You need to build the Accountability Loop.

The Accountability Loop is a cultural mechanism where standards are enforced continuously from every direction. In a weak organization, accountability only flows downward. The boss checks on the manager. The manager checks on the employee. This is exhausting. It scales poorly. It turns leaders into police officers.

In a high-trust organization, accountability flows in every direction. Leaders hold the team accountable. The team holds the leaders accountable. Most importantly, peers hold each other accountable. When the loop is closed, the culture defends itself.

Creating this loop requires absolute consistency. It requires the understanding that no task is too small and no team member is too high-level to fulfill basic responsibilities.

The fastest way to destroy the Accountability Loop is to introduce the VIP Exemption.

The VIP Exemption happens when a leader allows a top performer to bypass the basic rules of the organization. This is a trap that catches almost every business owner at some point. You have a brilliant engineer who writes flawless code. You have a charismatic salesperson who brings in double the revenue of anyone else. You have an executive who secures critical partnerships.

Because they produce massive results, you give them a pass on the small things.

They leave their dirty dishes in the breakroom sink. You say nothing. They skip the mandatory internal training sessions. You look the other way. They are rude to the administrative staff. You justify it by pointing to their quarterly numbers.

You tell yourself that you are making a strategic compromise. You tell yourself that you cannot afford to upset your top producer over something as trivial as an unreturned shopping cart.

You are wrong. You cannot afford not to.

When you grant a VIP Exemption, you instantly shatter the trust of your entire team. You send a loud, undeniable message that your core values are fake. You prove that your standards are actually negotiable. You teach your organization that bad character is acceptable as long as the revenue is high.

Cart Finishers despise hypocrisy. They operate from deep internal standards. When they see you tolerate sloppy, arrogant, or dismissive behavior from a top performer, their respect for you drops to zero. They will not complain. They will simply start looking for another job. You will lose your most reliable, ethical people because you were too scared to confront one high-producing Cart Abandoner.

I once consulted for a specialized manufacturing firm that fell into this trap. They had a lead designer who was a genius. His product designs were the lifeblood of the company. He was also incredibly arrogant.

He refused to document his workflow in the shared company portal. This was a basic administrative requirement for every employee. It ensured that if someone was sick or away, another team member could seamlessly pick up the project. The designer felt this task was beneath him. He claimed he was too busy innovating to fill out forms.

The CEO let it slide. He was terrified the designer would quit and take his talent to a competitor.

The fallout was predictable and severe. Within two months, the junior designers stopped documenting their work. When confronted, they pointed directly to the lead designer. The project managers became frustrated because they could not track progress. Communication broke down. Deadlines were missed. The entire production cycle slowed to a crawl.

The CEO tried to enforce the rule on the junior staff while continuing to exempt the lead designer. The staff revolted. They recognized the double standard immediately. The culture turned toxic.

The problem was never the shared portal: the problem was the broken Accountability Loop. The CEO allowed status to dictate responsibility.

You cannot preach attention to detail and let your highest-paid executive ignore typos. You cannot preach respect and let your top salesperson talk down to the receptionist. You cannot preach ownership and let your senior partner walk past a mess on the floor.

If the rules do not apply to your best people, you do not have rules: you have suggestions.

To build a closed Accountability Loop, you must hold your highest performers to the highest behavioral standards. You must demand that the people with the most authority exhibit the most humility. When a new hire sees the company president put their coffee mug in the dishwasher, the standard is set. When the new hire sees the top sales executive stop to pick up a stray piece of paper in the lobby, the standard is cemented.

No one is above the baseline.

Once you eliminate the VIP Exemption, you pave the way for peer-to-peer accountability. This is the highest level of operational health.

Peer-to-peer accountability happens when team members correct each other without needing a manager to intervene. It is the moment a junior associate reminds a peer to double-check their report before submitting it. It is the moment a team member quietly tells a colleague to clean up their workspace. It is the moment the group refuses to tolerate a Cart Drifter in their ranks.

You cannot force peer-to-peer accountability into existence. You have to cultivate the conditions for it to grow.

The first condition is clarity. Your team must know exactly what the baseline is. They must know what a returned cart looks like in every area of your business. If the standard is vague, no one will defend it. You must define what constitutes a finished job. You must define what acceptable communication looks like. You must define how the physical environment should be maintained.

The second condition is a combination of professional respect and high expectations. Your team must feel confident enough to speak up, but driven enough to care. They need to know that correcting a peer is an act of loyalty to the team, not an act of hostility.

You foster this by modeling how to deliver small corrections.

Leaders often make the mistake of saving all their feedback for formal performance reviews. They watch small details slip for six months. They document the failures. Then they drop a heavy critique on the employee in a closed-door meeting. This creates defensiveness. It creates fear.

To build the Accountability Loop, you must make corrections small, fast, and direct.

Do not wait for an annual review. Address the drift the moment you see it. If someone submits a report with sloppy formatting, hand it back immediately. If someone leaves a mess in the conference room, call them back to clean it up.

Keep your tone neutral. Keep the correction brief.

You do not need to give a lecture on integrity. You simply redirect the behavior back to the baseline. You say, "We do not submit reports with these errors. Please fix this and return it." You say, "We leave this room cleaner than we found it. Please grab those cups."

When you correct small things quickly and without anger, you normalize accountability. You remove the sting. You teach your team that feedback is just data used to maintain the standard.

When your team sees you consistently correcting small deviations without creating drama, they will begin to do it themselves. They will realize that holding the line is everyone's job.

They will also begin to hold you accountable.

This is the final, most crucial stage of the loop. You must invite your team to call you out when you miss a detail. You are human. You will occasionally leave your metaphorical cart in the lot. You will get rushed. You will drop the ball on a minor responsibility.

When this happens, how do you react?

If a junior employee points out that you forgot to log your notes in the CRM, do you get defensive? Do you remind them of your title? Do you brush them off because you are busy?

If you do, you destroy the loop. You prove that accountability only flows downward.

When a team member catches your mistake, you must thank them. You must fix the error immediately. You must publicly acknowledge that they were right to call you out. This is how you prove that the standard is bigger than your ego. This is how you prove that the company relies on mutual enforcement.

Building the Accountability Loop is not complicated, but it is difficult. It requires vigilance. It requires you to have uncomfortable conversations. It requires you to confront the top performers you would rather leave alone.

Are you willing to do that?

Look at your current team. Who is currently operating under a VIP Exemption? Who is allowed to ignore the small details because of their tenure, their title, or their talent?

You must confront that behavior today. You must sit them down and reset the expectation. You must explain that their results do not excuse them from the cultural baseline. If they push back, let them. If they threaten to leave, hold the door open for them. Your culture is worth more than their individual production.

Next, audit your feedback mechanism. Are you waiting too long to correct minor drift? Are you letting the carts pile up before you say something?

Start making small, fast corrections. Normalize the process of keeping the environment clean. Remove the emotion from the feedback. Treat accountability as a daily routine, not a rare disciplinary event.

Finally, ask your team to hold you to the same standard. Tell them explicitly that you expect them to call out your mistakes. When they test you, pass the test. Own your failures. Fix them fast.

A business without an Accountability Loop is a business built on an unsustainable foundation. It relies entirely on your energy to keep it standing. When you are tired, the business suffers. When you are absent, the standards fall.

A business with a strong Accountability Loop is a fortress. It polices itself. It naturally repels Cart Abandoners. It attracts and retains Cart Finishers. It allows you to step away, knowing that the people inside will continue to do the right thing simply because that is the way things are done.

Close the loop. Remove the exemptions. Make accountability a shared responsibility. The standard is only as strong as your willingness to defend it.

Chapter 7: The ROI of Reliability

The ROI of Reliability

Return on investment is a concept usually reserved for finance, marketing, and operational efficiency. You spend a dollar on a new software system, and you expect to save two dollars in administrative time. You invest a thousand dollars in an advertising campaign, and you expect to generate five thousand dollars in new revenue. We track these metrics obsessively. We build spreadsheets to monitor them. We hold meetings to discuss them.

Yet, we rarely apply this same rigorous math to human behavior.

Reliability is not just a soft skill. It is a financial metric. When you hire someone, partner with someone, or promote someone, you are making an investment. You are investing capital, time, and trust. The return on that investment is entirely dependent on their character. High-trust individuals generate a massive, compounding return. They give you your time back. They protect your reputation. They solve problems before those problems reach your desk. Unreliable individuals do the opposite. They drain your resources. They require constant management. They create operational drag.

In this chapter, we will look at the tangible business benefits of building a team based on the Shopping Cart Test. We will move beyond the theory of good behavior and examine the exact mechanisms of how trust translates to speed, efficiency, and profit. Small actions scale. When you hire people who consistently return their shopping carts, your entire business moves faster.

The Friction of Low Trust

Friction is the resistance that one surface encounters when moving over another. In physics, friction slows things down. It generates heat. It wears down machinery. If you do not oil the gears, the engine eventually stops working.

In business, friction is the resistance created by unreliable people.

Every missed email is friction. Every late arrival is friction. Every minor oversight, forgotten attachment, and poorly communicated update is friction. On their own, these moments seem trivial. You might excuse them. You might tell yourself that the person was just busy or distracted. But these moments are not isolated incidents. They are the data points of a pattern. When you tolerate these patterns, you introduce friction into the core machinery of your business.

Think about the daily operations of your company. How much of your day is spent managing people who should be managing themselves?

You assign a task to a team member. You wonder if it will be done on time. You write a follow-up email to check their progress. You wait for their reply. You finally receive the work. You find a mistake they should have caught. You send it back for revisions. You wait again.

This is the friction of low trust.

Compare that to a high-trust environment. You assign a task to a team member. You completely forget about it. They deliver the finished work on time, exactly as promised.

The difference between those two scenarios is not just peace of mind. It is measurable time and money. When you have to verify someone's work constantly, you are paying a hidden tax. I call this the management tax. If you hire someone to do a job, but you have to spend three hours a week checking their work, you have not bought your time back. You have simply purchased a second job. You have become an expensive babysitter.

I experienced this friction firsthand early in my career. I worked with someone who handled big ideas incredibly well. They could pitch a vision. They could strategize about the future. They were charismatic and persuasive. But they consistently overlooked small responsibilities.

They were a classic Cart Drifter. They would leave their cart in the middle of the parking lot and expect someone else to clean up the mess. In our business, this behavior showed up in their daily habits. They missed emails. They left tasks incomplete. They made minor oversights in client proposals. At first, I ignored these signals. I told myself that visionaries are not detail-oriented. I rationalized their behavior because they brought other skills to the table.

That was a mistake.

Eventually, those small issues created massive delays. A missed email turned into a frustrated client. An incomplete task meant another team member had to work late to finish it. The minor oversights required me to review everything this person produced. My schedule became clogged with their unreturned shopping carts. The friction they introduced slowed down the entire operation. It cost us time. It cost us momentum. Most importantly, it cost us trust with our clients.

The big ideas did not matter because the small details were failing.

When you hire people who lack reliability in the small things, you are not just accepting minor inconveniences. You are institutionalizing low standards.

Many leaders fail to realize how quickly this friction spreads. Low trust does not operate in a vacuum. It infects the entire team. What happens when your reliable employees see an unreliable employee getting away with missed deadlines and sloppy work?

They notice. They always notice.

The reliable employees resent the unreliable ones. They resent having to pick up the slack. They resent having to double-check the shared documents. They resent having to apologize to clients for mistakes they did not make. But more dangerously, they begin to resent you. They watch you tolerate low standards. They see you accept excuses. They realize that your stated values do not match your accepted behaviors.

When you allow friction to exist, you punish your best people. You force your Cart Finishers to clean up after your Cart Drifters. Over time, your best people will stop trying so hard. They will lower their own standards to match the environment. Or, they will simply leave and find a leader who demands excellence.

Friction also fundamentally changes how a business operates. When trust is low, companies build bureaucracy to compensate.

Why do companies have ten-step approval processes for a simple purchase? Because someone abused the company credit card. Why do companies have rigid, minute-by-minute tracking software? Because someone lied about their working hours. Why do companies require three managers to sign off on a basic client email? Because someone previously sent out an email with an embarrassing error.

Rules are the administrative evidence of failed trust.

When you cannot trust the people you hire to do the right thing instinctively, you have to create policies to force them to do it. You build guardrails. You add checkpoints. You require status meetings. Every single one of these additions slows down the business. They require administrative overhead. They require management bandwidth. They stifle agility.

Competitors who operate with high-trust teams do not need these checkpoints. They move fast. They make decisions quickly. They execute without endless meetings. They win because they do not have the drag coefficient of unreliable personnel holding them back.

This brings us to the actual financial cost of low trust.

Are you calculating the true cost of unreliability in your business?

A late arrival is not just five minutes of lost time. It is the disrupted focus of the five other people sitting in the meeting room waiting for the latecomer. A slow response to a prospect is not just a delayed email. It is a lost contract because the competitor replied an hour earlier. A minor spelling error in a presentation is not just a typo. It is the immediate loss of credibility in the eyes of a million-dollar client.

People who excuse small failures do not understand how business works. The marketplace does not care about your intentions. It only cares about your execution. If your team cannot execute the small details flawlessly, the marketplace will assume you cannot handle the major projects.

Look at your own calendar right now. Look at your communication channels. Where is the friction?

Who on your team requires the most follow-up? Who consistently brings you problems instead of solutions? Who do you implicitly trust to handle a client crisis without your supervision? Who makes you feel anxious when they are assigned a critical task?

The answers to these questions will reveal the ROI of your hiring decisions.

You cannot afford to keep people who generate friction. The cost is too high. The emotional drain on your leadership energy is too heavy. You only have a finite amount of cognitive bandwidth each day. If you spend that bandwidth worrying about whether an employee actually sent the email they promised to send, you have nothing left for strategic growth.

High-trust individuals operate from internal standards. They do not need you to remind them to follow up. They do not need you to proofread their work. They take ownership of their environment. They return the shopping cart because it is the right thing to do, not because you are watching.

When you fill your company with these types of people, the friction disappears. The business glides. Your bottom line improves not because you invented a new product, but because you stopped wasting money managing bad behavior.

Audit your team today. Identify the sources of friction. Have the hard conversations. Set the standard. Unreliable behavior is a choice, and your tolerance of it is also a choice. Choose to eliminate the friction. Make reliability your highest operational priority, and watch how quickly your business accelerates.

Predicting the Future

Business leaders love to predict the future. We build complex financial models to forecast quarterly revenue. We run market simulations to anticipate consumer trends. We hire specialized analysts to examine leading indicators in our sales pipeline. If a leading metric drops by two percent, we adjust our entire strategy immediately. We trust the numbers. We believe in the data.

Yet, when it comes to the people we hire, we abandon data completely. We rely on hope.

We hope the new senior manager will handle the stress of the third quarter. We hope the new vendor will deliver on their aggressive promises. We hope the junior employee will not cut corners when the deadline approaches.

Hope is not a business strategy. It is not a reliable method for building a high-trust team. You do not need hope to predict how someone will behave under pressure. You need a behavioral data set.

Human behavior is remarkably consistent. People run on patterns. The problem is not that human beings are unpredictable. The problem is that we choose to look at the wrong data.

We look at the candidate's resume. We look at their behavior in a structured interview. We look at their rehearsed presentation. These are not genuine data points of character. They are performances. When people know they are being evaluated, they wear a mask. They say the right things. They project total competence. They show you the most polished, artificial version of themselves. You cannot base your operational predictions on the mask. You must base your predictions on what happens when the mask slips.

This is why small, unguarded behaviors are the most accurate forecasting tool you possess. When someone thinks no one is watching, they revert to their baseline. When the stakes are low, they operate from their true internal standards.

There is a dangerous myth in the corporate world. It is the belief that people will suddenly change their nature when the stakes are high.

We see a minor flaw in a candidate before we hire them. They are slightly disorganized in their email replies. They miss a small detail on an assessment. They offer a weak excuse for arriving a few minutes late. We notice the behavior, but we brush it off. We tell ourselves that it was just a small task. We assume they will focus harder when the million-dollar account is actually on the line.

This is a fundamental misunderstanding of human nature. People do not change their nature for big events. They fall to the level of their habits.

High pressure does not create new skills or forge better character. High pressure simply amplifies what is already there. Pressure requires cognitive energy. It removes the extra energy required to maintain a professional mask. When the deadline is tight and the client is angry, an unreliable person will not suddenly become meticulous. They will panic. They will cut corners. They will look for someone else to blame.

If someone cannot manage the small details when the environment is calm, they will fail to manage the major details when the environment is chaotic.

Years ago, I considered partnering with an external marketing agency. Their formal pitch was brilliant. Their portfolio was impressive. The founders were charismatic and spoke about their commitment to excellence. I was ready to sign a long-term contract.

Instead of signing immediately, I proposed a small, low-stakes pilot project. It was a basic campaign that required minimal resources. I wanted to see how they operated in the real world before I handed over significant capital.

During the pilot, the agency missed a scheduled check-in call. The account manager emailed me three hours later with a casual apology about a calendar mix-up. A week later, they delivered the initial draft of the campaign. It was generally good, but it contained two glaring formatting errors. They were small mistakes. They did not ruin the campaign. But they were visibly careless.

I brought the errors to the attention of the agency founder. He minimized them. He told me that his team was currently prioritizing their larger clients. He promised that once we signed the primary contract, his team would bring their absolute best focus to our account.

He thought he was reassuring me. He was giving me all the data I needed.

I declined the contract. I knew that if they tolerated sloppy work on a test project specifically designed to win my business, their baseline standards were low. They were telling me exactly how they would treat my account once the initial excitement ended. If doing the right thing was too much effort when the stakes were small, it would be impossible when the stakes were high.

I used current small behaviors to forecast future performance. That simple observation saved me thousands of dollars and months of operational frustration.

You must learn to translate minor actions into major predictions. Every small behavior correlates to a larger business outcome.

Consider how someone handles a borrowed item. If an employee borrows a reference book from your desk and returns it a month later, dog-eared and stained, you have learned something vital. You have learned that they do not respect assets that do not belong to them. How will they treat the company budget? How will they manage a corporate credit card? They will treat your money exactly how they treated your book.

Consider how someone speaks about their former colleagues. If a candidate spends ten minutes of an interview gossiping about the incompetence of their previous boss, they are giving you a precise forecast. They are showing you their default method for handling professional conflict. When they inevitably disagree with your decisions, they will not address the issue with you directly. They will complain about you to the rest of your team.

Consider a minor exaggeration. A potential partner slightly inflates a harmless metric during a casual conversation. You know the real number, and you know they are stretching the truth to look better. It seems harmless in the moment. But what is the forecast? They have just proven that their integrity is conditional. If they will bend the truth when there is nothing to gain, they will fabricate the data when their quarterly bonus is on the line.

Consider the shopping cart. A person finishes loading their groceries. It is raining slightly. The cart return is forty feet away. They leave the cart propped up on a curb and drive away quickly.

What is the forecast?

They have demonstrated that when a task is slightly inconvenient, they will abandon it. They have demonstrated that they expect someone else to clean up the mess they created. In business, this translates directly to project management. When a project hits a difficult roadblock at five o'clock on a Friday, this person will not push through to solve the issue.

They will leave the metaphorical cart on the curb. They will log off, go home, and let you deal with the angry client on Monday morning.

Forecasting requires you to pay attention. Most business owners miss these signals because they are not actively looking for them. You must turn yourself into a disciplined observer of patterns.

Do not look at one single action and pass permanent judgment. Look for the baseline. Look for the repetition.

Does the prospect always arrive exactly one minute late? Does the vendor consistently take two full days to reply to a simple question? Does your junior manager always have a perfectly crafted excuse for why a target was missed?

Excuses are a particularly strong data point. High-trust individuals take absolute ownership of their failures. Unreliable individuals distribute the blame. If someone blames the traffic, the software, or a coworker for a minor delay today, they will blame the market, the algorithm, or your leadership for a massive failure tomorrow.

The data is always there. You just have to stop ignoring it.

Think about the worst hiring mistake you ever made. Think about the strategic partnership that ended in a bitter, expensive dispute. Think about the employee you had to fire for a serious breach of trust.

Were you truly surprised?

If you look back honestly, you will realize you were not surprised at all. The signals were there from the very beginning. You saw the early signs of entitlement. You noticed the minor inconsistencies in their stories. You felt a brief flash of hesitation when they failed to follow through on a simple request during their first week.

You saw the data. You just chose to rationalize it.

You told yourself that no one is perfect. You told yourself that their technical skills outweighed their behavioral quirks. You prioritized the convenience of filling a role over the character required to execute the role. You lied to yourself because addressing the behavior in the moment felt like too much work.

Trusting the wrong person is rarely a true surprise in hindsight. It is simply the inevitable result of ignoring the forecast.

You cannot change a person's baseline standards. You can train an employee to use a new software system. You can teach a salesperson your specific closing framework. You cannot teach an adult to care about the details when you are not in the room.

Character is established long before a candidate walks into your office. Your job as a leader is not to fix them. Your job is to read them.

Start treating small behaviors with the operational seriousness they deserve. Track the unreturned emails. Note the minor exaggerations. Watch how they treat the receptionist in the lobby. Watch how they react to mild, unexpected inconvenience.

Gather the data. Trust the pattern. Make your decisions based on the cold reality of their actions, not the warm potential of their words.

When you use small behaviors to predict the future, the future becomes much more profitable. You stop hiring liabilities. You start hiring assets. You build a resilient team that can carry the heavy weight of high-stakes pressure because they have already proven their strength in the low-stakes moments. Forecast accurately, and you will dramatically reduce your risk. Stop waiting to see what happens. Look at what they are already doing, and act accordingly.

The Compound Interest of Character

Compound interest is a mathematical certainty. If you leverage it, you build wealth. If you ignore it, you pay the price.

We understand this mathematical principle perfectly in finance. You invest a small amount of money consistently. Over time, the interest builds on the principal. Then the interest builds on the interest. The growth curve starts flat. Eventually, it goes vertical. A minor, consistent investment turns into massive wealth.

This exact same mathematical principle applies to human behavior. Character compounds.

When you hire a high-trust individual, you do not just get the value of their daily labor. You get the compounding return of their consistency. Every time they follow through on a promise, they add to the principal. Every time they return the shopping cart, they generate interest. Over months and years, this consistent behavior builds a wall of trust.

Now look at the opposite. Unreliability also compounds. It works exactly like high-interest debt.

You hire someone who constantly cuts corners. They miss a small detail. You pay the penalty of correcting it. They arrive late to a meeting. You pay the penalty of lost momentum. They alienate a coworker. You pay the penalty of reduced team morale.

Soon, you are spending all your operational profits just paying down the interest on their bad habits. Your leadership energy is drained by the massive debt of their unreliability.

Business owners constantly fall into a specific trap when trying to build their teams. They try to buy a shortcut. They look at the market, see the competition, and decide they need an immediate edge. So, they hire exclusively for credentials.

They look for the Ivy League degree. They look for the tenures at prestigious firms. They prioritize the polished resume over the behavioral baseline. They assume that high credentials automatically equal high performance.

This is a massive miscalculation.

Credentials are a static asset. They do not grow. A degree from a top university means someone passed a rigorous test ten years ago. It tells you nothing about what they will do when a client sends an angry email at four o'clock on a Friday. It tells you nothing about their willingness to do the unglamorous work required to keep a business running. High credentials without high character represent a structural failure.

How exactly does character compound in a business setting? It starts with the smallest possible interactions.

Watch the lifecycle of reliability. A new employee takes notes during an internal meeting. They organize those notes. They send a concise summary to the team before anyone asks for it. The action takes five minutes. On its own, it is a minor efficiency.

But watch what happens next. The manager realizes they do not need to check on this employee. The manager reallocates their mental bandwidth to a bigger problem. The employee is given a slightly larger responsibility. They handle that responsibility with the exact same level of meticulous care. They do not complain. They do not let the small details slip.

The manager begins to trust them implicitly. The client notices. The client realizes that whenever this specific employee is on the email thread, things get done accurately. The client stops worrying. The client stops asking for updates. The client gives your company more of their business.

This is the compound interest of character. A five-minute habit of taking notes turned into a lucrative, long-term client relationship.

You cannot put a credential on a resume that generates that kind of return. You can only earn it through repeated action.

In business, a competitive advantage is usually defined by intellectual property, capital, or market share. But these things are fragile. A competitor can raise more capital. A competitor can reverse-engineer your product. A competitor can undercut your pricing.

There is one thing a competitor cannot steal. They cannot steal the compounding trust you have built with your market through reliable behavior.

When your team executes flawlessly on the small things, you create a protective barrier around your business. Competitors with higher credentials but lower standards cannot cross that barrier. Why? Because the marketplace is exhausted by unreliability.

Your clients are tired of being over-promised and under-delivered. Your vendors are tired of chasing late invoices. Your partners are tired of reading sloppy proposals. When you provide an environment of absolute reliability, you become indispensable. People will pay a premium to work with you. They will ignore a cheaper competitor. They will ignore a flashier competitor. They will stay with you because you do not create friction in their lives. You remove it.

I saw this dynamic play out when I needed to secure a new logistics vendor for a critical project. The stakes were high. I narrowed the choice down to two finalists.

One was a massive, multinational firm. They had the slickest presentation I had ever seen. Their executives wore expensive suits. They casually dropped the names of Fortune 500 companies they had worked with. They handed me a glossy, hundred-page proposal. They possessed every credential you could possibly want on paper.

The other was a regional firm. Their presentation was straightforward. They did not have famous clients. But they did have a peculiar habit. Every single time I asked them a question during our vetting process, they responded within thirty minutes. When they said they would call at two o'clock, my phone rang at exactly two o'clock. When I asked for an obscure piece of insurance documentation, they provided it perfectly formatted in a single file.

I gave the contract to the regional firm.

My colleagues thought I was making a mistake by passing up the prestige of the multinational firm. But I was not buying prestige. I was buying reliability.

Over the next two years, this vendor handled hundreds of critical shipments for us. They never missed a deadline. They never lost a package. When a sudden winter storm shut down a major delivery route, their account manager called me at six in the morning with a backup plan already in place. They solved the problem before I even knew the problem existed.

Meanwhile, I watched my competitors who had hired the prestigious firm struggle. That firm was so big they did not care about the small details. They missed delivery windows. They sent confusing invoices. Their account managers were impossible to reach during emergencies. My competitors had bought the credential. I had bought the character.

The compounding return of that reliability saved my company an immeasurable amount of time and stress. They gave us a massive operational advantage. We could move faster and promise more to our own clients because we knew our foundation was solid.

Reliability creates margin. Margin is the breathing room in your business.

When you operate with low-trust individuals, you have no margin. Everything is an emergency. A missed deadline creates a cascading failure across five different departments. You live in a constant state of reaction. Your business becomes brittle.

High-trust individuals absorb chaos. They are the structural integrity of your company. Because they manage the small details perfectly, they prevent small problems from becoming large emergencies. This gives you the margin to think. It gives you the margin to strategize. It gives you the margin to innovate.

You cannot build a visionary company if you are constantly managing preventable emergencies started by sloppy employees. Look at the most successful companies in any industry. They are not always the companies with the most brilliant ideas. They are usually the companies with the highest standards of execution.

When FedEx promises to deliver a package, they deliver it. When Amazon says an item will arrive on Tuesday, it arrives on Tuesday. When a professional services firm handles a complex filing with zero errors, they win the next contract. They do the mundane things perfectly. They return the shopping cart. They answer the phone. They double-check the math. They tell the truth. The market rewards this consistency with fierce loyalty.

Why do leaders fail to prioritize this? Pride.

Leaders want to brag about their hires. It sounds better at a dinner party to say you hired a former executive from a tech giant than to say you hired a steady, meticulous worker from an unknown regional firm. We let our ego dictate our business decisions. We want the shiny object.

But the shiny object loses its appeal quickly if it lacks substance. You cannot build a business on bragging rights. You can only build a business on execution.

If you want a true competitive advantage, you must remove your pride from the equation. You must stop valuing what looks good and start valuing what actually works. What works is consistency. What works is character. What works is the quiet, unglamorous habit of doing exactly what you said you would do, every single time.

Do you want to win the long game? Do you want to build an organization that outlasts your daily supervision?

Stop chasing the highest pedigree. Start chasing the highest baseline. Hire the person who replies to emails promptly. Hire the person who formats the spreadsheet correctly. Hire the person who picks up the trash in the hallway when no one is looking.

Do not ignore these small behaviors. Do not treat them as nice bonuses. Treat them as the core requirements of employment. When a candidate shows you that they hold themselves to a high internal standard, hire them immediately. Give them resources. Give them authority. Let their character compound within your organization.

Evaluate your current team today through the lens of compound interest. Who is generating a positive return through their daily reliability? Who is acting like high-interest debt, draining your time and resources through their constant need for supervision? You must make the hard choice to eliminate the debt. Cut the unreliable performers, regardless of how impressive their resumes might be. Reinvest your capital and your trust into the people who do the small things right. Make consistency your highest metric, and watch your competitive advantage multiply.

Chapter 8: Building a Trust-Based Future

Building a Trust-Based Future

Building a business is ultimately an exercise in building trust. You have spent the previous chapters learning how to decode the small, everyday behaviors that reveal true character. You know how to spot the difference between a Cart Finisher and a Cart Drifter. You understand why interviews are fundamentally flawed and why reputation often masks a lack of reliability. You have the tools to read people accurately. Now, the challenge is maintaining that standard over the long term. Trust is not a one-time achievement. It is a continuous practice. This final chapter will show you how to embed the Shopping Cart Test into the DNA of your business and your life.

Refining Your Behavioral Intuition

As your business scales, your time becomes your most heavily taxed resource. You move from doing the work to managing the people who do the work. Eventually, you move to managing the managers. At each level of growth, the distance between you and the daily operations increases. This distance creates a massive vulnerability.

When you are busy, the first thing you abandon is your attention to detail. You start looking at the broad strokes. You read the executive summary. You look at the quarterly revenue. You stop watching the small behaviors. This is exactly when your business is most at risk.

You will feel a strong temptation to outsource your judgment. You will want to rely on the screening process of an external recruiting firm. You will want to lean on the impressive bullet points on a candidate's resume. You will want to assume that because someone held a senior title at a known company, they possess the character required to succeed in yours. That assumption is a trap. You can delegate tasks, but you can never delegate your responsibility for setting and enforcing behavioral standards. The moment you stop paying attention to how people act in the small moments, you lose control of your company culture.

People often refer to their "gut feeling" about a person. They interview a candidate or sit down with a potential partner and leave the room feeling uneasy. They cannot point to a specific flaw in the business plan. They cannot find an error in the resume. Yet, something feels off. They dismiss this feeling as irrational intuition.

It is not irrational at all. Intuition is simply rapid pattern recognition. Your brain processed a small behavior that contradicted the polished narrative you were being sold. You noticed a subtle shift in eye contact when a specific question was asked. You observed a dismissive tone used toward an assistant. You saw a brief flash of arrogance when a mistake was pointed out. You did not consciously register the detail, but your brain recognized the pattern.

Refining your behavioral intuition requires bringing these unconscious observations into your conscious awareness. You must keep your sniper's lens sharp. You do not achieve this by watching everyone all the time. That is micromanagement, and it is entirely unscalable. You achieve this by paying extreme attention during specific, unguarded moments.

You must look at the edges of an interaction. How does the person behave in the five minutes before the meeting officially begins? How do they act in the parking lot? How do they respond when a minor technical glitch interrupts their presentation? These transitional spaces are where the mask slips. High-trust individuals remain consistent across all environments. Low-trust individuals perform when the spotlight is on and relax their standards when they think no one is looking.

Let me give you a concrete example of how trusting this intuition pays off. Years ago, I needed to fill a crucial operational role. The stack of applications was full of impressive credentials. One candidate, however, did not have the exact background I thought I wanted. On paper, they lacked the polished pedigree of the other applicants. But my intuition told me to pay attention to their behavior. I noticed they were the only person who arrived exactly ten minutes early. I noticed how they structured their follow-up emails. The messages were clear, precise, and devoid of fluff. I gave them a small, seemingly insignificant task during the interview process. I asked them to send over a specific document in a specific format by a specific time. They executed it perfectly.

I gave this reliable unknown the opportunity over the more "qualified" individuals. I hired them based on the consistent, high-standard behavior I observed in those low-stakes moments. They showed up early, communicated clearly, and did exactly what they said they would do. Over time, they entirely outperformed the individuals with better resumes. They did not just do their job. They anticipated problems. They took ownership. They were a Cart Finisher in every sense of the word. If I had relied solely on the traditional metrics of hiring, I would have missed out on one of the best team members I ever had. Your intuition, grounded in the observation of small behaviors, will often point you toward the right people that conventional metrics overlook.

To keep your behavioral intuition sharp as you get busier, you must systematize your observation. You cannot rely on chance encounters to see how people behave. You must design small tests into your standard operating procedures. This does not mean playing games with people. It means creating deliberate opportunities for their true character to surface before you make a major commitment.

When interviewing a candidate, take them on a walk through the office. Drop a piece of paper on the floor in front of them. Do they step over it, or do they pick it up? Take them out for a cup of coffee. Watch how they treat the barista. Better yet, get their coffee order wrong on purpose. How do they react to a minor inconvenience? Do they become visibly irritated, or do they handle it with grace? These small scenarios replicate the Shopping Cart Test in different environments. They provide a window into the person's baseline level of entitlement, ownership, and composure.

You can apply this same systematic observation to your existing team. Assign a minor, slightly tedious task that falls just outside their formal job description. Watch how they handle the request. Do they complain that it is not their job? Do they rush through it and deliver sloppy work? Or do they apply the same level of care and precision as they would to a major project? Remember my core belief. How someone handles minor responsibilities is exactly how they will handle major ones. If they cannot manage a simple administrative task with excellence, they will inevitably drop the ball when managing a high-stakes client account.

The single biggest threat to your behavioral intuition is your own desire for convenience. This is the rationalization trap.

You desperately need to fill a leadership role. You find a candidate with a stellar track record. They have the exact industry experience you need. They have the relationships. They have the polish. But during the final interview, they make a subtle, disparaging comment about a former colleague. Or they show up late and offer an excuse instead of an apology. Your sniper's lens catches the signal. Your intuition flares up. You know this is a red flag.

Then the rationalization begins. You tell yourself it was just an off day. You tell yourself the comment was just a bad joke. You tell yourself you can manage their personality because you need their skills. You ignore the behavioral signal because starting the search over is highly inconvenient. You prioritize immediate relief over long-term reliability.

This is a guaranteed path to failure. When you ignore your behavioral intuition for the sake of convenience, you are actively choosing to invite a problem into your business. You must train yourself to believe what you see the first time. When someone shows you they have low standards in small things, you must accept that this is exactly who they are. Do not try to separate the behavior from the person. The behavior is the person. A single red flag in a low-stakes environment is a preview of a massive failure in a high-stakes environment.

You must build the discipline to walk away. Walking away from a seemingly perfect deal or a highly qualified candidate because of a small behavioral flaw is incredibly difficult. It requires total confidence in your observation and absolute conviction in your standards. But every time you compromise your standards for convenience, you weaken your culture. You signal to the rest of your team that character is secondary to capability. Over time, that compromise will erode the foundation of trust in your organization.

Refining your intuition also requires constant calibration. As your business evolves, the context of your decisions will change. The behaviors that defined success in your first year might look different than the behaviors required in your tenth year. You must continuously observe the high-trust individuals currently in your life to understand what excellence looks like in your current environment.

Look closely at the people who consistently deliver results without creating drama. What are their micro-behaviors? How do they communicate delays? How do they respond to critical feedback? How do they handle the transition between complex projects?

By studying the small actions of the most reliable people you know, you create a behavioral baseline. You build a mental database of what right looks like.

When you have a clear, internalized picture of high-trust behavior, low-trust behavior becomes glaringly obvious. You will no longer need to analyze every interaction deeply. You will simply recognize when someone deviates from the baseline. This is the ultimate goal of refining your behavioral intuition. It is about making the observation of character an automatic, effortless process.

Your time is your most valuable asset. You cannot afford to spend it micromanaging people who lack internal standards. You cannot afford to waste it untangling the messes created by individuals who cannot be trusted with the small things. By trusting your observations, systematizing your tests, and refusing to rationalize bad behavior, you protect your time and your business. The sharper your lens, the faster you can filter out the liabilities. The faster you filter out the liabilities, the sooner you can focus on scaling your business with people who consistently do the right thing.

The Zero-Tolerance for Small Failures

When you hear the phrase "zero-tolerance", you might think of a rigid, unforgiving corporate policy. You might picture a workplace where people are terrified of making a single mistake. That is not what I am advocating. You must draw a hard line between a gap in skill and a gap in character.

A skill gap happens when an employee misconfigures a new software program. A skill gap happens when a new hire fumbles a client presentation because they are nervous. You should have infinite patience for skill gaps. You train for them. You coach people through them. You give your team the room to learn, fail, and improve.

A character gap is entirely different. A character gap happens when that same employee misconfigures the software and blames a junior colleague to save face. A character gap happens when a manager repeatedly shaves ten minutes off their timesheet. A character gap happens when someone acts entitled, dismissive, or dishonest in a low-stakes environment.

You must have zero tolerance for character gaps. You must stop waiting for a big failure to validate what a small failure already told you.

Most leaders hesitate to enforce standards on small things. They feel petty calling out a minor lie. They feel unreasonable firing someone over a seemingly insignificant breach of protocol. They tell themselves they are being too demanding. They tell themselves they need to wait for a "real" offense before taking action.

This hesitation is dangerous. Character does not suddenly change when the stakes get higher. It simply scales. The person who lies about a fifty-dollar expense report will lie about a fifty-thousand-dollar budget deficit. The stakes change. The behavior pattern remains exactly the same.

You have to understand the underlying psychology of a small failure. When someone chooses to cut a corner in a low-stakes moment, they are revealing their baseline standard. They are showing you what they do when they believe there are no consequences. High-trust individuals do not calculate when to have integrity. They operate from a fixed internal standard. Low-trust individuals perform a constant cost-benefit analysis. They do the right thing only when the risk of getting caught is high.

When you tolerate a small failure of character, you validate their cost-benefit analysis. You teach them that their low standards are acceptable in your environment. You give them permission to test the boundaries further.

This boundary-testing is exactly how major corporate disasters begin. No company wakes up one morning to find out an executive embezzled millions of dollars without prior warning signs. No business loses its top three clients overnight due to poor service without a long trail of ignored red flags. If you trace any major business failure back to its origin, you will find a series of small, tolerated character breaches.

This trap is especially common for early-stage companies and growing startups. When you are desperately trying to scale, you prioritize speed over everything else. You need bodies in seats. You need someone to manage the overflowing inbox. You need a vendor to ship parts tomorrow. In this state of desperation, you will ignore glaring behavioral failures simply to keep the machine moving. You are trading your long-term security for short-term relief. That trade will always bankrupt your culture.

You are the gatekeeper of your business. If you want to build a high-trust future, you must learn to sever ties before the catastrophic failure occurs.

The hardest place to apply this principle is with your top performers. Every business owner faces this dilemma eventually. You have a salesperson who shatters every revenue target. They bring in massive accounts. They are charming, aggressive, and undeniably effective. But they also fail the small tests constantly. They are rude to the administrative staff. They consistently bend compliance rules. They withhold critical information from their peers to maintain a competitive advantage.

Your rational brain will work overtime to justify keeping them. You will look at the revenue they generate. You will calculate the cost of replacing them. You will convince yourself that their technical ability outweighs their behavioral flaws. You will tell yourself that you can isolate them from the rest of the team.

You cannot isolate toxicity. It always leaks.

When you keep a toxic high performer, you send a devastating message to the rest of your organization. You tell your reliable, high-trust employees that character is just a marketing slogan. You prove that results excuse bad behavior. Your Cart Finishers will watch the top performer get away with cutting corners. They will realize that their own integrity is undervalued. Eventually, your best people will leave. You will be left with a culture populated entirely by opportunists.

You have to make the difficult decision to pivot or part ways. You must fire the brilliant jerk. You must cut ties with the lucrative partner who lacks ethics. You must do this even when it hurts your bottom line in the short term.

Let me share a scenario where I learned this the hard way. Early in my career, I was negotiating a joint venture with a highly successful consultant. This partnership was projected to double our regional revenue within twelve months. The consultant had the network, the industry knowledge, and the operational capacity we needed.

We met for a final dinner to sign the paperwork. It was a celebratory, low-stakes environment. Halfway through the meal, the server accidentally spilled a few drops of water on the table while refilling our glasses. It was a harmless mistake. The consultant immediately berated the server. He used a demeaning tone, insulted the server's intelligence, and demanded a manager.

My intuition screamed at me. I was watching a textbook failure of a small behavioral test. This person felt comfortable abusing power when dealing with someone they deemed unimportant.

I ignored the signal. I rationalized it. I told myself he was just stressed about the deal. I told myself his behavior at a restaurant had nothing to do with his ability to execute our business plan. I wanted the revenue, so I signed the contract.

Seven months later, the joint venture imploded. The consultant applied that exact same dismissive, abusive behavior to our shared clients whenever a minor disagreement arose. He alienated three of our largest accounts. He belittled my team members. He refused to take accountability for missed deliverables. The partnership cost us far more in lost reputation and client churn than it ever generated in revenue.

The failure was not a surprise. The signal was clear from the very beginning. I simply lacked the discipline to act on it. I failed to apply zero-tolerance to a small character breach.

You must do better. You must build the conviction to act on the patterns you see.

When you decide to part ways with someone over a pattern of small failures, you will face severe pushback. The individual will accuse you of being unfair. They will point out that they hit all their metrics. They will demand to know exactly what major rule they broke.

You must be prepared for this conversation. You do not need to win an argument. You simply need to state the facts about their behavior.

You look them in the eye and say, "We require a specific standard of ownership and collaboration here. Over the past three months, I have observed a consistent pattern where you blame others for missed deadlines. You have repeatedly dismissed feedback from your peers. This behavior does not align with the foundation of trust we require to operate."

They will argue that these were minor incidents. They will claim they were just joking or that others are too sensitive. Do not engage in a debate about the scale of the failure. Reiterate that the pattern of behavior is the issue. You are not parting ways because of one missed deadline. You are parting ways because they refuse to take responsibility for their actions.

Applying zero-tolerance to small failures also requires you to look critically at your external partnerships. Trust extends beyond your payroll. It includes your vendors, your suppliers, and your strategic partners.

If a vendor consistently sends invoices with accidental overcharges, you must fire them. It does not matter if they quickly correct the invoice when you catch it. The pattern indicates a lack of internal standards. If they will cheat you on a minor supply order, they will abandon you during a major supply chain crisis.

If a strategic partner repeatedly reschedules meetings at the last minute without apology, you must reevaluate the relationship. Reliability is a habit. Someone who does not respect your time in low-stakes planning sessions will not respect your capital in high-stakes executions.

Enforcing this zero-tolerance policy will feel painful at first. You will experience short-term disruptions. You might have to step back in to cover a vacant role. You might have to rebuild a vendor relationship from scratch. You might lose a client who is tied to a toxic salesperson.

Embrace the disruption. The short-term pain of enforcing your standards is always less severe than the long-term agony of managing low-trust individuals.

When you consistently remove people who fail the small tests, a profound shift happens in your business. Your operations become incredibly efficient. You no longer spend hours mediating petty disputes. You no longer have to double-check every report for hidden errors. You no longer waste energy wondering if your partners are operating in good faith.

More importantly, your high-trust employees will notice. They will see that you protect the environment. They will see that you value character over convenience. This builds deep, unwavering loyalty. High performers thrive in environments where standards are strictly maintained. They want to work with other highly reliable individuals. By eliminating the liabilities, you create a space where true talent can flourish.

Takeaway: Do not wait for a catastrophic failure to make a personnel decision. Small lapses in integrity, ownership, and respect are not anomalies. They are accurate previews of future behavior. Adopt a zero-tolerance policy for patterns of low character. Protect your business by acting decisively on the small signals.

Beyond the Cart

You have spent the duration of this book learning how to filter the people in your business. You know how to identify high-trust employees. You know how to spot the early warning signs of a toxic partner. You understand the financial and operational return on reliability. But your business does not exist in a vacuum. Your business is an extension of your life. If you apply the Shopping Cart Test strictly at the office but abandon it the moment you walk out the door, you will eventually fail.

Character does not clock out at five in the evening. Character is not a uniform you wear to the office and take off on the weekends. It is singular. It is permanent. The person who cuts corners in their personal life will eventually cut corners in your shared business endeavors.

Many leaders create an imaginary wall between their professional standards and their personal relationships. They demand absolute accountability from their sales team. They refuse to tolerate missed deadlines from their vendors. Yet, they spend their weekends surrounded by friends who constantly break promises. They maintain relationships with people who lie, gossip, and operate with massive entitlement.

This creates a dangerous cognitive dissonance. You cannot be a hardline defender of integrity in the boardroom while acting as an enabler of bad behavior in your living room. Eventually, the chaos of your personal life will bleed into your professional life.

You must understand that your energy is a finite resource. As a business owner, your mental clarity is your most valuable tool. When you surround yourself with low-trust individuals in your personal life, they drain that clarity. You spend your weekends managing petty drama. You waste emotional energy trying to decode the passive-aggressive text messages of an unreliable friend. You exhaust yourself making backup plans because you know a family member will likely flake on a commitment.

Every ounce of energy you spend managing the unreliability of your personal network is energy stolen directly from your business. You cannot lead a high-performing team on a Monday if your weekend was consumed by low-trust individuals.

Applying the Shopping Cart Test to your personal life requires the exact same sniper lens you use in business. You must look at the low-stakes social interactions. You must observe how people handle minor obligations when there is no financial contract binding them.

Pay attention to how people handle shared expenses. This is a classic behavioral test. When you go out to dinner with a group, watch what happens when the bill arrives. High-trust individuals take immediate ownership. They calculate their share. They offer to cover the tip. They ensure the group is not left short. Low-trust individuals perform a different routine. They conveniently step away to take a phone call. They underpay their portion by a few dollars. They promise to send you the money later and then force you to remind them three times before they actually do it.

Do not dismiss this as a mere annoyance. It is not about the five dollars they failed to tip. It is about their internal standard. They are comfortable letting others carry their weight. If someone is willing to exploit a friend over a restaurant bill, they lack the foundational integrity required for true trust.

Watch how people treat borrowed items. If a friend asks to borrow a book, a tool, or a piece of equipment, you have just handed them a test. A high-trust individual treats borrowed property better than their own. They return the book in pristine condition. They return the tool clean and ready to use. Most importantly, they return it without you having to ask for it. They recognize that borrowing an item creates a minor debt of trust, and they are eager to clear that debt.

A low-trust individual will keep the item indefinitely. They will wait for you to ask for it back. When you finally do ask, they will act as if you are inconveniencing them. They might return the item damaged and offer a casual excuse instead of a replacement. This behavior reveals a deep lack of respect for boundaries and ownership. It is the exact same mindset of the person who leaves a shopping cart in the middle of a parking space. They believe their convenience is more important than your property.

Punctuality in personal settings is another massive indicator of character. In business, people are often on time because their paycheck depends on it. In personal relationships, punctuality is driven entirely by internal respect. When someone consistently shows up late to dinner reservations, social gatherings, or casual meetups, they are sending a clear signal. They are telling you that their time is inherently more valuable than yours. They will offer a constant stream of excuses. Traffic was bad. Their alarm did not go off. They got caught up in an email.

Stop listening to the excuses. Look at the pattern. If they value the relationship, they will manage their time. If they are consistently late, they do not respect you. It is that simple.

Let me offer an example of how ignoring these personal signals can cost you deeply. Years ago, I had a close friend I will call Mark. We had known each other since college. We shared the same social circle and spent a lot of time together. Mark was fun to be around, but he constantly failed the small behavioral tests. He would borrow a cooler for a weekend trip and return it three weeks later, unwashed. He would commit to helping a mutual friend move an apartment, only to cancel the morning of the move with a vague excuse. He routinely parked his car blocking the sidewalk in front of his house, forcing pedestrians to walk into the street.

I saw all these behaviors. My intuition registered them. But I rationalized them. I told myself that Mark was just a bit scattered. I told myself that his lack of organization was just part of his charm. Because he was a friend, I lowered my standards.

A few years later, I decided to start a new business venture. I needed a partner to handle the marketing and outreach. Mark had recently left his job in that exact field. It seemed like a perfect fit. We had a long history. We trusted each other. I brought him in as an equal partner.

It was a total disaster. The exact behaviors I had tolerated in our friendship immediately surfaced in our business. The unwashed cooler became ignored client emails. The canceled moving help became missed vendor deadlines. The entitled parking habit became a total refusal to take accountability for his mistakes. He was exactly who he had always been. The stakes simply got higher. I had to spend months legally untangling him from the business, costing me thousands of dollars and nearly destroying the company before it even launched.

I did not have the right to be surprised. Mark had been showing me his true character for years. He had failed the personal Shopping Cart Test hundreds of times. I simply chose to ignore the results because of our shared history.

This brings us to a difficult but necessary step. If you want to build a high-trust future, you must prune your personal network. You must stop investing time in people who consistently demonstrate low standards.

Many people fall into the trap of shared history. They maintain toxic friendships simply because they have known the person for a decade. Time is a terrible metric for trust. The fact that you sat next to someone in high school does not obligate you to tolerate their lack of integrity today. You are not required to keep a seat at your table for someone who constantly disrespects your time, your property, or your boundaries.

Pruning your network does not require a dramatic confrontation. You do not need to call a meeting to announce you are ending a friendship. You simply need to restrict access. Stop initiating contact with people who drain your energy. Stop inviting the habitually late friend to important events. Stop lending money to the friend who never pays the bill. As you stop feeding the low-trust relationships, they will naturally wither.

This process will feel uncomfortable. You will feel a sense of guilt. You will worry that you are being too rigid or unyielding. Push through that discomfort. You are not being rigid. You are protecting your environment. You are enforcing the boundaries required to operate at a high level.

As you remove the low-trust individuals from your life, you create space for something incredible. You create space for a network composed entirely of Cart Finishers.

Imagine a personal life where every promise is kept. Imagine a social circle where you never have to double-check a plan, remind someone of a debt, or decode a passive-aggressive comment. Imagine the immense peace of mind that comes from knowing the people around you operate with the same high standards you demand of yourself.

This is the ultimate ROI of the Shopping Cart Test. When you surround yourself with highly reliable individuals in your personal life, your baseline of normal changes. Excellence becomes the default. You no longer waste time managing friction. You can engage in deep, meaningful conversations. You can bounce complex business ideas off your friends, knowing they will give you honest, grounded feedback. You can rest on the weekends, knowing your personal foundation is secure.

The people in your inner circle are the ones who will support you when your business faces a crisis. They are the ones who will celebrate your massive wins without jealousy. They are the ones you might eventually hire, partner with, or recommend to others. You cannot afford to populate this circle with people who cut corners.

The standard you walk past is the standard you accept. This is true in the warehouse. It is true in the boardroom. It is true in your dining room.

You have the tools to read behavior. You understand the profound difference between words and patterns. You know that no integrity decision is ever small. Now, you must make the commitment to live by these principles.

Look at the people in your life right now. Watch what they do when no one is forcing them to do the right thing. Observe the small, unguarded moments. Trust your intuition when it spots a red flag. Stop rationalizing bad behavior for the sake of convenience or shared history. Demand reliability from your team, and demand it from your friends.

Building a high-trust future is not a destination you reach. It is a daily practice. It is a relentless commitment to observing behavior, enforcing standards, and refusing to compromise on character. The signals are everywhere. The test is always happening. Keep your lens sharp, trust what you see, and build a life with the people who consistently return the cart.

Takeaway: Your personal relationships dictate your professional capacity. Tolerating low-trust behavior in your private life drains the energy required to build a high-trust business. Apply your behavioral standards universally. Restrict access to individuals who fail the small tests, and aggressively build a personal circle composed entirely of highly reliable people.

Connect with Author

Connect with Michael JP Wilson

https://linktr.ee/michaeljpwilson